T0195910

G R A C E

THE GOSPEL OF THE KINGDOM OF GOD

NORMAN WILSON

authorHOUSE®

AuthorHouse™
1663 Liberty Drive
Bloomington, IN 47403
www.authorhouse.com
Phone: 1-800-839-8640

Published by AuthorHouse   10/10/2014

ISBN: 978-1-4969-4640-9 (sc)
ISBN: 978-1-4969-4639-3 (e)

CONTENTS

Introduction

The purpose of this book is to provide those family members and friends who have faithfully prayed for me and supported me in my quest for grace with a written copy of the treasures I have discovered. My prayer is that it will help guide its readers into a greater understanding of the grace of God and a deeper appreciation of the unconditional love of God for them. The content of this book has been accumulated through many hours of pleasure discovering the treasures of the Kingdom of God and the Gospel of grace.

Some of what I share is not original with me but has been gleaned from the writings and teachings of many great men of God; men who not only taught grace but also expressed it through their lives. I readily give credit to all who have helped me gain a greater understanding of grace by sharing the treasures they themselves have discovered. I have no desire to claim their revelations as mine but to give credit for their valuable input in my search for a greater understanding of grace. Other family members and friends have taught me grace through the way they responded to the issues and difficulties of life. The names of those who have enriched my life with their teachings of grace are too numerous to mention. Many I recall, but others who contributed through a sentence, concept, or nugget that uncovered a truth and gave me greater understanding regarding grace, I am unable to recall and give due credit. Ultimately I must give credit to the Holy Spirit who prompted me to attend sessions, listen to C/Ds, and read books by godly teachers and preachers of grace. He gave me revelation and understanding of the truths that I received from these sources and guided me in formulating my present understanding of the gospel of grace. I realize that I have only scratched the surface of this wonderful topic and look forward to continuing this exciting journey of finding and extracting nuggets of truth from the scriptures as unveiled by the Author. The ongoing challenge is the process of internalizing these truths and expressing them in life situations.

The study of the true gospel of grace by its very nature confronts those areas in the modern church that insist Christians must abide by the law of the Old Covenant or some mixture of law and grace. The scriptural definition of true grace will also challenge the practice of pseudo-grace. If one is to fully enjoy the benefits of true grace it is necessary to identify and avoid these erroneous teachings.

This does not diminish the value of the true Church or its local congregations. The Church is not the Kingdom but is a valuable asset of the Kingdom. The Church provides the opportunity for passionate worship of God to be expressed. It is through the Church that God provides guidance, power, healing, miracles and other expressions of His grace. The Church will not be perfect because its very goal is to help its members through the process of maturation.

I realize that for some these writings may challenge your present theology and provide an entirely new way of examining scriptures. Others may outright disagree with these writings. I acknowledge their right to do so. However, if you are reading this book you obviously have a high regard for scripture and are searching for the truth. Therefore, I encourage you to read with an open mind and search the scriptures for yourselves as the Bereans did in response to Paul's teaching of grace. (Acts 17:11)

CHAPTER ONE

The Essence of the Kingdom of God

God created from nothing the invisible spiritual domain called Heaven with all its angelic beings. As Creator, everything He creates belongs to Him, and He exercises control, authority and power over His creation. This realm of His rule, authority, and influence where He alone rules supremely over all things is called the Kingdom of God. Divine forensics will show that every created thing has His trademark on it. It all belongs to Him, and He assumes responsibility for the welfare of all created beings and things related to His Kingdom.

The essence of this Kingdom is the very character of God. When God created His Kingdom, He purposed that it would be a kingdom of grace, goodness, mercy, compassion, love, forgiveness, healing, deliverance, and all the characteristics of His person. God desired that this essence be expressed and experienced in the physical portion of His Kingdom. The result is, whenever there is an expression of any of these attributes, goodness, kindness, forgiveness, mercy, genuine love, etc. this is an expression of the aspects of the Kingdom.

God created man in His own image to rule over the physical portion of His kingdom and to express the essence of His Kingdom. The created purpose of man was to represent God by exercising rule over portions of His Kingdom.

> *"Then God said, "Let Us make man in Our image, according to Our likeness, let them have dominion over the fish of the sea, over the birds of the air, and over the cattle, over all the earth and over every creeping thing that creeps on the earth." Genesis 1:26*

When God created Adam He designed his entire being-body, soul and spirit- to be the operative through which He could manifest the essence of the Kingdom of God. Adam's total being was designed to function in harmony with all aspects of the Kingdom. God breathed into him, and Adam became a living, active being with the capacity to reveal the essence of the Kingdom of God. Adam's role was to express the heart of God and His Kingdom in the physical world in which he lived. When Adam disobeyed God and ate of the tree of the knowledge of good and evil, his spirit died and he forfeited his ability to manifest the concepts and essence of the Kingdom.

All men born after the fall of Adam were still designed by God to house the essence of the Kingdom but lacked the spiritual nature of God to manifest it. They now possessed a lower sinful nature that was incapable of expressing the essence of the Kingdom. This sinful nature was handed down from Adam through the genetic bloodline, so it passed down to all mankind.

God restored man's ability to once again be able to express the characteristics of the Kingdom through the birth of His Son by the Holy Spirit and the Virgin Mary. Jesus was birthed by the Holy Spirit, not an earthly father and was born without a sinful nature. Jesus, as the second Adam, accurately presented the nature and heart of God and the essence of His Kingdom. The Kingdom could not come until Jesus came and demonstrated the essence of the Kingdom by a life that accurately described what the Father was like and thereby provided Christians with the example of how to manifest the Kingdom. Jesus was the personification of the Kingdom because His entire being- body, soul, and spirit was totally in harmony with the nature of the Father.

At the beginning of His earthly ministry Jesus was anointed with the Holy Spirit on the day He was baptized. This enabled Him to present the Kingdom in all its power, generosity, and compassion. From that day He began to preach that the Kingdom was at hand because He was at hand. He began to teach and demonstrate the concepts, precepts, guidelines, rules, principles, and instructions of the Kingdom.

From Adam to the coming of Christ, the Spirit, who is the Essence of the Kingdom, was only given in measure to certain individuals so they could demonstrate an aspect of the Kingdom. Now, when a person is born again, his spirit becomes one with the Holy Spirit and he becomes capable of presenting the characteristics of the Kingdom to a lost world.

When Jesus had completed His earthly ministry making it possible for men to be indwelt by the Spirit and nature of the Kingdom, He told His disciples that it was necessary for Him to return to heaven so that He could send the Holy Spirit. He commanded them to wait until the Holy Spirit came and provided them with the power to be His witnesses. He ascended to the right hand of the Father where He released the Holy Spirit on the day of Pentecost. The Holy Spirit Himself is the Kingdom in all its manifestation. Paul wrote that the Kingdom of God is not eating and drinking but righteousness and peace and joy IN THE HOLY SPIRIT. He is the essence, the nature of the Kingdom. To be filled with the Spirit is to be filled with the Kingdom (Romans 14:17, Acts 1:8, Acts 2:33).

Different types of perfumes are created by a mixture of ingredients which produce their individual aromas. These aromas are not the essence but are a product of the mixture, which is the essence; so it is with the Kingdom. The external functions and actions of the Kingdom such as love, compassion, kindness, healing, deliverance, etc., are only the manifestations of the internal essence of the Kingdom.

The Kingdom may be likened to leaven or yeast which is placed in dough to change the nature of the dough into bread. The Holy Spirit is placed within us to enable us to release the essence of the Kingdom. He does this by conforming us daily to the image of Christ. Just as a grain of corn placed into the ground will die and come back alive in a new form, the Christian placed into Christ dies and becomes a new creation with a divine nature capable of expressing the nature of the Kingdom.

Computers have hard drives capable of storing many gigabytes of programs for activity. The hard drive can only express its internal programs through a monitor. The monitor cannot house or activate the programs; it can only reflect what is happening. If a computer does not have a particular program on the hard drive, it cannot perform the functions of that program. In the same manner, we can only express externally what is internalized within us. We can only express the attributes of the Kingdom to the degree that they have become a part of our internal makeup. Sin, in most cases, can be defined as a violation of some ingredient of the Kingdom. Hatred violates the ingredient of love; bitterness is a violation of forgiveness; sickness is the absence of the wholeness desired and arranged for by a merciful God. Evil is the absence of goodness.

The Holy Spirit provides the individual with grace that enables him to express the essence of the Kingdom. When a person rejects the promptings or enabling of the Holy Spirit, he allows his flesh to control his actions and misrepresents the essence of the Kingdom. "But we have this treasure in earthen vessels, that the excellence of the power may be of God and not of us" (2 Corinthians 5:7).

CHAPTER TWO

Defining grace

I realized in my early years as a minister that I was not a preacher. Although I have preached, I do not possess the gifting and calling of a preacher. Preachers have messages on their heart which address problem areas in the Christian life and offer biblical solutions. My gifting is teaching. I don't apologize for that because I believe every gift in the body of Christ is important. My heart is to discover the nuggets and treasures in the written word of God and share them in a manner that is easily understood in their application. I believe, when these truths are received and acted upon, they will indeed set us free from the bondage of unbiblical thinking. The Scriptures are the compass that guides us through the mazes of life. I treasure the Scriptures as God's message to mankind and would do nothing deliberately to misuse them.

While I attempt to define grace I readily confess that my knowledge of grace exceeds my application of grace in certain areas. That is to say I have not fully internalized all areas of grace. Learning to adjust our lives and activities to who God says we are, and exercise the grace that He provides, is a life long process. It is my desire to grow in the grace and knowledge of our Lord and Savior Jesus Christ and to be a grace representative in my world (2 Peter 3:18).

Many of you have experienced those "aha" moments when you were reading a particular verse in the Bible, or heard a preacher or teacher comment on a verse, and a light came on and you said, "Oh, that is what that means, and it goes with this verse and these verses". I have had many of those in my Christian life, but the ones that have impacted my life the most came through reading a book that a friend gave me titled "Destined to Reign". It was written by a preacher of grace from Singapore, by the name of Joseph Prince. As I began reading this book, the truths of many vague scriptures, as well as many familiar scriptures came alive with new understanding. I experienced a series of aha moments to the extent that I could scarcely put the book down. I used my Bible to verify the content and context of the scriptures that Prince used, and found them very enlightening. I finished the book with a totally new outlook about the grace of God.

The book keenly whetted my appetite to learn more about grace. So I began ordering and reading books by other grace writers such as Andrew Wormmack, Andrew Farley, Steve McVey, Rob and Ryan Rufus, Andre van der Merwe, Tullian Tchividjian and many others. These writers all expressed basically the same truths about grace, but added their personal revelations. I began to examine scripture with a new eagerness, and the more I studied about grace, the more I found there was to study. I am sure that I have just touched the tip of the iceberg, so to speak, but am excited about discovering new nuggets with each study.

An understanding of the Kingdom of God is essential to every believer because it is the realm through which God exhibits the gospel of grace. The Kingdom of God is alive with holy activity and is ever expanding. The Holy Spirit expresses new emphasis of the gospel of the Kingdom by highlighting it on a global basis. Often times this emphasis will challenge our paradigms, (those beliefs that influence the decisions and activities of our lives), and we may have to adjust our biblical beliefs accordingly.

Whenever God wishes to emphasize something in His Kingdom, He does it on a global scale through the Church. The Church is the Bride of Christ, and He loves and reveals His heart to her. It is through the Church that He desires to release power and miracles, to effect healing, and to teach the aspects of these emphases as they relate to His Kingdom.

Currently I believe the Spirit's emphasis is on the New Testament gospel of grace. Not that there has never been an emphasis on grace, for grace was a major teaching of New Testament writers. However, through the process of trickle down theology, the clear lines between the Law and grace have become so intertwined that the purity of the gospel of grace has been compromised. This is not a new trend but one that has plagued the Church through the centuries from the inception of the Church. Paul confronted it in the churches he established. The church at Jerusalem was still greatly influenced by it, as witnessed by Paul's reception during his third visit to Jerusalem many years after his conversion. It also was the cause for his rebuke of Peter at Antioch (Galatians 2:11-13).

The root of this error insists that even though one is saved by grace, he must still follow certain aspects of the Law. This mixture of grace and Law has been embraced and included in the doctrines of churches through the ages. In its core it maintains that we are saved by grace, but we must maintain our righteousness through good works. Once embraced, this error was sanctioned and taught in many denominational seminaries where future church leaders prepare for ministries. These performance-based doctrines, which stress self-help plans designed to assist members in attaining something that God has declared they already possess, have been adopted by many local congregations. These churches then develop sin management programs that include lists of requirements for Christians to follow. One such requirement is that a Christian must confess his/her sins to be forgiven and cleansed by God. This is often done as a means to assist members in becoming better persons, when what it actually does is place them in bondage to the law.

Leaders that embrace the message of grace seem to fall into four categories. First are those that give mental assent to the gospel message, but believe that because they do not preach the Law, they are preaching grace. They may spend hours studying each week and be able to articulate with flowing words the content of scripture to their congregations. While these messages may contain valuable truths, the good news of the gospel of grace may never be expressed. It is interesting to hear about the historical events of the lives and times of biblical characters, but unless these truths are linked to the grace of God, they remain just good-to-know historical facts. Second are those that fear if they preach grace in its truest form, their congregation will depart from the disciplines that motivate them not to sin. So they take the facets of grace and make them into rules of performance, which is the essence of the Law. Third are those that fully understand the redeeming grace of God and preach it with passion. They preach the total forgiveness of sin and the unconditional love of God; that God through the death of Jesus on the cross punished all sins forever; that salvation is totally from God without help from man; that there is nothing man can do to save himself and that once a person receives salvation by a belief in Jesus there is nothing he can do to lose it. However, they fail to articulate the responsibilities that accompany becoming a child of God; responsibilities that have as their source the new nature of the person, not requirements. This leads some to conclude that, since their sins are all forgiven, they may indulge the desires of the flesh without accepting their responsibilities to God and others. This is a form of pseudo-grace. Fourth are those who preach the redeeming grace of God but also declare that the enabling grace of God equips a person to walk in his new nature and relate to others through acts of grace. They emphasize the wholeness of grace as shown by God to man and as shown by Christians to others. They stress relationships rather than performance. They maintain that what God says about them is true, that He desires to show them favor, and they are capable of living a victorious life over sin. The church or individual that wishes to truly express the grace of God will embrace this last holistic view of the gospel of grace.

Religion is another enemy of the Church because it causes distortion through its man-developed programs, and often pharisaical approach to the scriptures. Religion may be defined as any attempt to reach and please God or a god outside the gospel of grace. Although it disguises itself in many forms, it always includes the efforts of man to accomplish and maintain his own salvation. In the local church it may manifest in many ways, i.e., by mixing the requirement of the Old Covenant with the freedoms of the New Covenant. Examples of these practices include maintaining the Sabbath by worshipping on Saturday, by observing Jewish holidays, by wearing certain Jewish apparel, by embracing certain Jewish customs, and by abstaining from certain acts or foods. All of these are an attempt to gain favor from God and present an outward appearance of piety.

The Holy Spirit never emphasizes one aspect of the gospel while neglecting other equally important attributes of the Kingdom. Wherever grace is emphasized, it will always include such things as worship, giving, forgiveness, righteous living and love. The Spirit will never abandon nor weaken the old tried doctrines of the faith that have weathered skepticism though the years. Through this book I desire to share some of the nuggets of grace that I have discovered.

I believe there are four areas that assist in understanding the importance of the gospel of grace: (1) To define grace, (2) Our identity in Christ, (3) Differences between the Old and New Covenants and (4) How to rightly divide the word of truth as it relates to our responsibilities to the old and new covenants. I will address each of these in this and subsequent chapters.

To attempt to define grace is like trying to define God. No matter what we say about it, there is always more. Several years ago Dr. S.M. Lockridge preached a sermon titled, "That's my King". After using superlatives again and again to express the greatness of God, he makes a statement, "I wish I could describe Him to you". That is how I feel about defining grace.

In the sense that gospel means "good news" grace and gospel may be used interchangeably since they both encompass the fullness of God's love expressed to mankind. The scriptures contain many truths, but not all truth is good news. It is true that if one rejects the gospel he will go to Hell, but that is not good news. The good news is that God has made provisions through grace so that none have to go to Hell. True grace is always good news.

To try and explain true grace, a person must take into account that, in the Christian realm, there are as many definitions and beliefs about grace as there are individual Christians and local churches. Therefore, I will examine grace as it relates to the New Covenant.

If ten Christians were asked to define grace they would probably give the standard definitions, "God's unmerited favor" or an acronym, "God's riches at Christ's expense" and they would be right. But should you ask them what it means to them personally, you would get ten different definitions because they would describe their experiences with the grace of God, and they would all be similar but different. So what I am sharing is my definition of grace, but it in no way covers all the aspects of grace. Grace is like the air we breathe. We may not understand how God designed the lungs to take in air, extract the oxygen, and exhale carbon dioxide, but we know without it we would die.

Our Bible is divided into two parts, the Old Testament and the New Testament. This is by God's design because they represent two major covenants. Testament means covenant so the Bible is divided into two covenants, the old and the new. It is important for us to understand our relationship with each of these covenants.

The Old Covenant is a composite of laws consisting of 613 requirements including the Ten Commandments, dietary laws, moral laws, civil laws and sacrificial laws. These are often referred to in the scriptures as the Law. These laws governed Israel's relationship with God. When they obeyed the Law they were blessed, and when they failed to obey they were punished and cursed.

Because the Law is a composite if you violate one law then you are guilty of violating them all or if you are committed to keeping one then you must keep them all. There is no picking and choosing which ones to keep.

James 2:10 – For whoever shall keep the whole law, and yet stumble in one point, he is guilty of all

Galatians 5:3 – And I testify again to every man who becomes circumcised that he is a debtor to keep the whole law.

In the same manner, the New Covenant of grace is a composite because it includes all of the goodness of God. The noun "grace" identifies all the goodness of God. The verb "grace" identifies the individual expressions of God's goodness, i.e. His love, mercy, kindness, forgiveness, provisions, protection, healing, and His relationship with His people. Whether expressed by God or individuals, these are expressions of grace.

Grace is similar to a red velvet cake. The cake is a composite of flour, eggs, sugar, milk and flavoring all mixed together to become a red velvet cake. It is now a composite of all its ingredients so if you eat a small piece or a large piece it will taste the same because it is all red velvet cake. In the same manner anytime you experience the goodness of God you are experiencing the grace of God. Whether you experience a small portion or a large portion it all tastes the same. It's all grace.

In some circles the teaching of grace has caused a negative reaction among Christians because it has been wrongly presented or misunderstood. The teaching of pure radical grace will confront many of the beliefs that we have been taught because it rests upon all that Christ has done, not on what we must do. If grace is presented in such a way that it causes Christians to believe that it is alright to sin or neglect their Christian responsibilities this is not grace; this is a pseudo-grace. There are major differences between true grace and pseudo-grace. Pseudo-grace fails to work in the trenches, relationships, or in life's hard issues. True grace provides love, understanding and patience when faced with these issues. Pseudo-grace permits all manner of flesh indulgence while true grace empowers the person to walk in the Spirit. Pseudo-grace can only produce works of the flesh while true grace produces the fruit of the Spirit.

Grace may be understood from two aspects; redeeming grace and enabling grace. Others have identified these two aspects as legal grace and living grace or acceptance grace and empowerment grace. Regardless it is important that we understand each aspect. Failing to understand the difference will lead to confusion and error.

Redeeming grace: Redeeming grace is the all inclusive marvelous plan of God for the salvation of mankind. It was conceived by the Trinity before the foundation of the world. God, foreseeing the fall of Adam, with its effect upon all mankind, and man's inability to redeem himself, devised a plan that includes all mankind; a plan simple enough for all to receive. God even provides the grace and faith to participate in this marvelous plan. It involved Jesus coming to earth to accomplish all that would be required for man to once again have a relationship with God and participate in His Kingdom. This plan was consummated by Jesus' death on the cross, His resurrection, and ascension to perform His priestly duties in the Tabernacle not made by man. Man can participate in this plan by believing and trusting in the Son of God.

Every sin committed by every man, woman and child ever born, for all time was placed on Jesus while he hung on the cross. He became the noun sin as well as the verb sin. That is to say He became the sin principle (noun) which births and motivates all sinful activity (verb). Jesus bore the wages of all sin on our behalf. In Christ, all sin was judged by God and punished by His death, thereby appeasing the holy wrath of God against sin. When God's wrath had been satisfied and His plan for man's redemption was complete, Jesus cried out, "It is finished" If something is finished, it is finished!!

John 4:34 – Jesus said to them, "My food is to do the will of Him who sent Me, and to finish His work".

John 17:4 I have glorified You on the earth. I have finished the work which You have given Me to do.

John 19:30 – So when Jesus had received the sour wine, He said "It is finished!" And bowing His head, He gave up His spirit.

When Jesus said, "It is finished' what did it mean for mankind?

- That every condition for the redemption of mankind was completed.

- God's wrath was satisfied and He is no longer angry with mankind.

- The punishment for all sin had been satisfied and God had forgiven mankind for their sins and would no longer punish them for those sins.

- That the requirements of the Law had been fulfilled and Christians were no longer under is rule.

- The curses associated with the Law were removed and only blessing remained.

- We are reconciled to God. We are no longer alienated from Him.

- We are made acceptable to God. We no longer have to perform to be accepted.

- Man could be one with God in an eternal relationship

- That God would provide everything we need for life and godliness.

- That we can be part of God's family and enjoy a relationship with Him

This is not an exhaustive list of what He meant There is much, much more.

This is the redeeming grace of God. We cannot add anything to it nor can we take anything from it. It is the sovereign will of God. God had a grace covenant with Abraham and the only requirement of the covenant was for Abraham to believe. He believed and it was counted to him as righteousness. The only requirement for an individual under the New Covenant is to believe in God's Son and when he does he becomes a new creature with all the benefits of being in God's family. He is no longer under the old Law and does not have to submit to countless acts of performance to be accepted by God.

Enabling Grace: Enabling grace is the grace that God provides through the ministry of the Holy Spirit which enables us to become all that God says we are and to accomplish all that He calls us to do. Grace is not passive. It is the expression of God's goodness. The following scriptures show the need for and results of enabling grace.

- Acts 1:8 – But you shall receive power when the Holy Spirit has come upon you; and you shall be witnesses to Me in Jerusalem, and in all Judea and Samaria, and to the end of the world.

- Ephesians 2:10 – For we are His workmanship created in Christ Jesus for good works, which God prepared beforehand that we should walk in them.

- Philippians 2:13 – for it is God who works in you both to will and to do for His good pleasure

- Philippians 1:6 – Being confident of this very thing, that He who has begun a good work in you will complete it until the day of Jesus Christ.

- 2 Corinthians 5:18-19 – Now all things are of God, who has reconciled us to Himself through Jesus Christ, and has given us the ministry of reconciliation. 19- That is, that God was in Christ reconciling the world to Himself not imputing their trespasses to them, and has committed to us the word of reconciliation.

- Philippians 4:13 – I can do all things through Christ who strengthens me.

- Romans 12:9-21 Paul outlines in these verses how a life in grace should look.

Redeeming grace births us into the family of God making us one spirit with Christ, declares us as righteous, and provides us with everything that pertains to life and godliness, and defines our identity in Him. Enabling grace provides us with the power and guidance to act like a child of God and to obtain all that is ours as heirs and joint heirs with Christ. Someone said, "Redeeming grace authorizes us to become a son of God; enabling grace provides us with the power to act like a son of God".

I wish I could describe it to you!

In summary, then, we can say that grace is a compilation of the immeasurable ways God expresses His goodness to mankind. It includes His unconditional love-a love that is not dependent upon our actions, good or bad; His mercy-His mercy is greater than His judgment. Mercy triumphs over Judgment (James 2:13, Proverbs 16:6); His goodness-God's glory is manifested through His goodness. The whole earth is filled with His glory because it is filled with His goodness. But the whole earth has yet to be filled with the knowledge of His glory. He has shared that glory with us. (Ex 33:18-19, Isa. 6:3, Hab. 2:14, Ps. 62:7, John 17:22); His forgiveness -Jesus' death on the cross was sufficient payment for ALL our sins, we are eternally forgiven of all sins. There will never be a need for another sacrifice because Jesus satisfied the judgment of the Law so our forgiveness is complete. Therefore, we can loudly declare with Paul, there is now no condemnation. God will never hold us accountable for what He has already punished Jesus for. His grace provides full forgiveness. His grace has also provided us with access to all manner of healing (Isaiah 53:4-5).

Grace is living every moment with the confidence that God loves us and desires to give us good things and do good things for us. "Every good gift and every perfect gift is from above, and comes down from the Father of lights, with whom there is no variation of shadow or turning" (James 1:17). "For the gifts and the calling of God are irrevocable" (Romans 11:29). "No good thing will He withhold from those who walk uprightly" (29 Psalms 84:11.)

Grace grants us access to the manifold provision of God needed in our daily life. "As His divine power has given to us all things that pertain to life and godliness, through the knowledge of Him who called us by glory and virtue" (2 Peter 1:3). Through the grace of God we have a divine nature. "by which have been given to us exceedingly great and precious promises, that through these you may be partakers of the divine nature, having escaped the corruption that is in the world through lust" (2 Peter 1:4). Grace enables us to accomplish everything He calls us to do. "I can do all things through Christ who strengthens me" (Philippians 4:13). (Emphasis mine)

By grace we have been relocated from the kingdom of darkness into the Kingdom of the Son of His love (Col 1:13). Since we have been transferred to the Kingdom of God's Son we become joint heirs with him, all the promises of the scriptures are ours and He promises to never leave us. (Romans 8:14-17, 2 Corinthians 1:19-22, Hebrews 13:5). Grace gives us access to our inheritance in Christ Jesus, everything that He bought for us on the cross, all the many wonderful promises, and things that He desires to give us (1 Corinthians 2:9).

Most biblical grace applications require a renewing of the mind. This is known as repenting, for to repent is to change the mind in regards to how we think about God and His Kingdom. To practice applications of grace, our minds must be renewed so that we believe God in those areas. For the mind to be properly renewed we must know and accept the biblical meaning of the application. The greatest motivator for applying grace principles in our daily lives is a love for God and for others. Our love for God grows out of a biblical understanding of who He is and what He has done for us. One of the greatest ways of showing love for God is through passionate worship of Him. A love for others grows out of our love for God and the understanding that what He has done for us He has also done for them.

Chapter Three

Developing our identity in Christ

In the garden the devil deceived Adam and Eve into believing that if they ate of the tree of the knowledge of good and evil they would become more like God. He insinuated there was something they could do to become more like God. They failed to realize they were already created in His image. Satan still uses that same approach on the church today. He deceives us into believing that there is a large variety of religious works that we must do to be accepted by God and be righteous like Him.

I spent a large portion of my Christian life trying to accomplish those things that would cause God to bless me and love me more. "Work out your own salvation" was my goal. But regardless of how much I did, it never seemed to be enough. I knew myself better than anyone, and I knew my sins and shortcomings. It seemed the harder I tried, the more I failed to live up to the Christian standards that I had been taught. I thought whatever the church required of me was what God required of me and knew I failed to measure up to these expectations. So I always lived under a cloud of guilt. I was confused and disappointed because the efforts that were supposed to make me better and produce joy were not working. I was reading and studying my Bible; I spent time in prayer, I participated in all church activities, even to the neglect of my family. All my efforts brought me no lasting pleasure or peace. I came to a place where I decided, since my efforts were not producing the expected results and satisfaction, I would leave the church and seek pleasure elsewhere.

I am grateful that God did not leave me in that state. Through His providence I attended a seminar where I learned the reason for my failures was that I was violating, even though unintentionally, many biblical principles. During the course of that seminar I was provided with biblical solutions that helped me make the necessary adjustments in my Christian walk. Although much of what I was taught involved a mixture of grace and Law the Holy Spirit used it to help me develop a more disciplined life and spend quality time with God. It was out of this time with God that He began to show me how to restructure my life according to the truths of His Word.

Like Adam and Eve, I was trying to become something that God already declared me to be. There were two contributing factors. First, I had a poor self image, because my identity was formed mostly from how I thought about myself, based upon my abilities and inabilities. This led to a performance based lifestyle, where achievement equaled acceptance and failure equaled non-acceptance. Secondly, I was mixing the requirements under the Old Covenant with the freedoms under the New Covenant.

An important factor of the Kingdom of God is for a person to believe what God says about them is true and structure their life accordingly. Who a person believes himself to be will dictate his actions, interests, creativity, values, beliefs, how he dresses, his choices and his relationships. When we develop or shape our identity from our performance, other's appraisal, our abilities, our looks, or our education, etc., we will have a distorted image of who we really are.

Our true identity should not be determined by what we can do or what others think about us, but by who God declares us to be. Being a doctor, lawyer, janitor, etc., does not define who we are, they identify what we do. This is very important because what we believe shapes our behavior. Changing our beliefs (renewing the mind Romans 12:2) will change our behavior.

- Matthew 4:17 – From that time Jesus began to preach and to say, "repent, for the kingdom of heaven is at hand".

- <u>Mark 1:15</u> – and saying "The time is fulfilled, and the kingdom of God is at hand. <u>Repent and believe in the gospel</u>".

True repentance has to do with changing our beliefs to align with God's Kingdom. Repentance is the first step in renewing the mind. The true meaning of repentance is to align the way we think with the truths of the scriptures (Proverbs 23:7 "as a man thinks in his heart so he is").

A person's significance and identity are greatly influenced by what the most significant person in his/her life declares them to be. Husbands and wives have the power to enhance their spouse's self-worth by what they say and how they treat each other. This is true in all relationships. When God is the most significant person in our lives, our self-worth and identity will be enhanced as we embrace what He declares about us. We find our true identity in what God declares about us. Believing what God says about us is renewing our mind.

- Philippians 2:5 – Let this mind be in you which was also in Christ Jesus.

<u>We are children of God</u>
- Romans 8:16 – The Spirit Himself bears witness with our spirit that we are children of God

- John 1:12 - But as many as received Him, to them He gave the right to become children of God, to those who believe in His name

<u>We have a divine nature</u>
- 2 Peter 1:4 – By which have been given to us exceedingly great and precious promises, that through these you may be partakers of the divine nature, having escaped the corruption that is in the world through lust

- 1 Corinthians 6:17 – But he who is joined to the Lord is one spirit with Him

We are the righteousness of God
- 2 Corinthians 5:21 –For He made Him who knew no sin to be sin for us, that we might become the righteousness of God in Him.

- Romans 3:22 – Even the righteousness of God, through faith in Jesus Christ, to all and on all who believe. For there is no difference.

- Romans 5:17 – For if by the one man's offense death reigned through the one, much more those who receive abundance of grace and of the *gift of righteousness* will reign in life through the One, Jesus Christ. (Emphasis mine)

We are saints not sinners
- 1 Corinthians 1:2 –To the church of God which is at Corinth, to those who are called to be saints, with all who in every place call on the name of Jesus

We are joint heirs with Christ
- Romans 8:17_– and if children, then heirs – heirs of God and joint heirs with Christ

- 2 Peter 1:3_As His divine power has given to us all things that pertain to life and godliness

- 2 Corinthians 1:20 – for all the promises of God in Him are Yes, and in Him Amen

We are forever secure in Him
- Ephesians 4:30 – And do not grieve the Holy Spirit of God, by whom you were sealed for the day of redemption

- 2 Corinthians 1:22 – who also has sealed us and given us the Spirit in our hearts as a guarantee.

The glory of God is upon us.
- John 17:22 – and the glory which You gave Me I have given them, that they may be one just as we are one.

<u>We must believe what God says about us is true and act like it.</u>

- James 1:23 – 25 – for if anyone is a hearer of the word and not a doer, he is like a man observing his natural face in a mirror. 24 -For he observes himself, goes away, and immediately forgets what kind of man he was, 25 - But he who looks into the perfect law of liberty (grace gospel) and continues in it, and is not a forgetful hearer but a doer of the work, this one will be blessed in what he does. (Emphasis mine)

The very intent of these verses is for one to look into the mirror of God's word and to see the image that God declares him to be and then live accordingly.

The following is an old story that has circulated through the years that illustrates how the influence of what the most significant person in our lives thinks about us helps develop our identity.

On an island in the South Pacific, it was the custom that when a young man intended to marry he would announce his intention of marriage to the entire village. After the announcement, he and the whole community would gather around the intended bride's home. Her father would come outside and then—in front of the community—the father and young man would barter over the price to be paid for the bride. The main item of value on the island was the cow. Therefore, a suitor would offer the father a certain number of cows for his daughter. The average bride was worth two cows, perhaps three if she was unusually bright or attractive. The all time record was four cows.

The most eligible bachelor on the island was Johnny Lingo. He was handsome and wealthy. Imagine all the excitement among the women of the island when Johnny announced one day that he had selected a wife. But then he shocked everyone by announcing that his choice was a girl named Serita. Serita was not even in the top ten of the most sought after young ladies. She was regarded as plain and frightfully shy. She had a poor self image and was not considered to be at all attractive. Some of the jokers in the crowd even suggested that Serita's father might pay Johnny a cow or two just to take her.

The community gathered at Serita's house for the bartering. What happened next was an even greater shock. Johnny's opening bid for Serita was eight cows! Her father almost fainted, but he managed to say yes. That very evening Johnny and Serita were married, and they departed for their home on an adjacent island.

For a full year no one saw Johnny and Serita. Then on their first anniversary they returned to visit their parents. From the moment they arrived at the dock, the news spread. Everybody said, "Come and see Johnny and Serita! You won't believe it!" Everybody came, but nobody noticed Johnny. All eyes were on Serita. She had been transformed! She was a vision of beauty and loveliness. She was poised, warm, friendly, and confident.

At the end of the day, as Johnny and Serita were preparing to return to their home, one of Johnny's longtime friends pulled him aside and said, "I want to know the secret of this amazing transformation in Serita. How did it happen?" Johnny said, "I will tell you. From the time Serita was born, she had been treated as though she was unattractive and not worth very much. She had begun to believe that about herself. But I announced to the community that she was an 8-cow wife, and I have treated her just that way. She has become that vision of herself that she sees every day in my eyes."

This story stresses the transformation that takes place when a person sees how the most significant person in their life views them, and they are transformed from the caterpillar they see themselves to be, into the beautiful butterfly that the other says they are. This is why it is so important for us to believe what God says about us and to structure our lives to match. In His eyes we are all more than 10 cow individuals.

We are all beautiful, intelligent, full of wisdom, creative, exactly how God designed us to be. Don't let the devil or others talk you out of who you really are in Christ.

CHAPTER FOUR

Understanding Covenants

The Bible reveals God as a covenant-making and covenant-keeping God. The Bible itself is a covenantal book divided into two sections, the Old and New Testaments (Covenants). Given the importance placed upon covenants in the Bible, it is difficult to understand why there is so little emphasis and teaching about covenants in the modern church.

The word "covenant" is mentioned 280 times in the Old Testament and 33 times in the New Testament. Covenants may be agreements between two individuals, between a king and his people, between God and individuals, and between God and groups of individuals. Some covenants are conditional while others are unconditional. When there are conditions, if one party violates or defaults on his part of the agreement the covenant is broken. Unconditional covenants do not require the recipient to meet certain conditions in order to receive the benefits of the covenant.

The Hebrew word for covenant is "Beriyth". It translates "to cut" hence a covenant is a "cutting" which refers to the cutting or dividing of an animal into two parts and the parties passing between the pieces to consummates the covenant (Genesis 15:17-18; Jeremiah 34:18. In the New Testament the Greek word for God initiated covenants is "Diatheke" which means "a disposition, arrangement, testament or will". In the Scriptures, when God is the initiator of a covenant, man can either accept it or reject it, but he cannot change it.

God's covenantal promise to Noah that He would never flood the earth again was unconditional, it required nothing from man. God's promise to David that one of his descendents would always be on the throne required no action on David's part. Jesus was the fulfillment of this promise because He was from David's tribe of Judah. God's covenant with Abraham was a conditional covenant. Abraham's only requirement was to believe God. When he believed God all the blessings of the covenant were his and it was accounted to him as righteousness. God's covenant with Israel was conditional in that it required both individual and nation to follow certain laws before they could receive God's blessings and avoid curses. An example of a covenant between individuals is the covenant between David and Jonathan (1 Samuel 18:1-4).

Abraham's Covenant: Genesis chapter twelve describes the ways God declares He will bless Abraham and in chapter fifteen God guarantees those blessings by making a covenant with him. This covenant eventually became a national covenant, as the descendents of Abraham became the nation of Israel. Through this covenant God expressed grace toward Abraham and his descendents. Their only requirement was to believe God.

- Abraham believed God and it was credited to him as righteousness (Romans 4:3). Righteousness is not defined as doing right but as right standing before God. This covenant has never been rescinded by God. The Old Covenant made on Mount Sinai was rescinded when the New Covenant of grace was initiated.

- Romans 4:13-15 (MSG)

"That famous promise God gave Abraham---that he and his children would possess the earth---was not given because of something Abraham did or would do. It was based on God's decision to put everything together for him, which Abraham then entered when he believed. If those who get what God gives them only get it by doing everything they are told to do and filling out all the right forms properly signed, that eliminates personal trust completely and turns the promise into an ironclad contract! That's not a holy promise; that's a business deal. A contract drawn up by a hard-nosed lawyer and with plenty of fine print only makes sure that you will never be able to collect. But if there is no contract in the first place, simply a promise---and God's promise at that---you can't break it".

Abraham's covenant of grace with God existed four hundred and thirty years prior to the giving of the Old Covenant containing the Law. Therefore, there were no penalties, curses or punishment associated with it. God never once chastised, cursed, punished, judged or showed displeasure with Abraham's behavior although Abraham did many wrong things. The covenant was not based upon Abraham's behavior but on the faithfulness of God. The only curses were for the enemies of Abraham. There is a similarity between God's covenant with Abraham and His covenant with Christians. Neither covenant places it's beneficiaries under the Law.

-   Rom 4:15 For the law brings about wrath (God's anger); for where there is no law there is no transgression.

-   Rom 5:13 ...but sin is not imputed when there is no Law.

-   Rom. 3:20 – Therefore by the deeds of the law no flesh will be justified in His sight, for by the law is the knowledge of sin.

All of Abraham's descendents were included in this grace covenant if they believed. This is important because, as Christians, we are also beneficiaries of this covenant, being spiritual descendants of Abraham

-   Galatians 3:26-29

For you are all sons of God through faith in Christ Jesus. [27] For as many of you as were baptized into Christ have put on Christ. [28] There is neither Jew nor Greek, there is neither slave nor free, there is neither male nor female; for you are all one in Christ Jesus. [29] And if you are Christ's then you are Abraham's seed (descendants), and heirs according to the promise. (Emphasis mine)

To understand the New Covenant of grace it is essential to understand the difference between our response to the Old Covenant of law and our response to the New Covenant of grace.

Old Covenant of the law. (Conditional)
- It was given to Moses on Mt Sinai on the first Pentecost after leaving Egypt. It was a covenant between God and Israel only, and did not apply to any gentile nation. (Amorites, Edomites, Moabites, Canaanites)

- It was terminated at the death of Jesus some 2,000 years ago therefore it never applied to any current gentile nation.

- It was written on tablets of stone (The New Covenant is written on hearts).

- It included 613 different laws that consisted of the Ten Commandments, dietary, civil, moral and sacrificial laws.

- It was a covenant of performance which contained both blessings and curses-blessings if the Law was obeyed and curses if it was not. (Deuteronomy 28:1-68). (14 verses regarding blessings, 54 regarding curses)

- Because it was conditional it could be and was broken by Israel many times.

- It was a ministry of death and condemnation because no one was able to keep its strict requirements. At the giving of the law 3,000 died because they broke the law only a short time after agreeing to keep it (Exodus 32:1-28, 2 Corinthians 3:6-8).

- It was given to identify acts and attitudes of sin (Galatians 3:19).

- God's purpose for the law was to show it was impossible for individuals with an old sinful nature to keep.

- Ezekiel 20:25 – Therefore I also gave them up to statutes that were not good, and judgments by which they could not live.

- (Galatians 3:10-14, James 2:10-11)

The Old Testament (Covenant) was terminated with the enactment of the New Testament (Covenant) on the first Pentecost after Jesus' death on Passover. Prior to Pentecost, Jesus was resurrected and ascended to the Tabernacle in Heaven, where He accomplished His priestly duties. Having done this, He sat down at the right hand of God as evidence that He had fulfilled His duties as our High Priest. When the Old Covenant of law was enacted 3,000 souls died. When the New Covenant of grace was enacted 3,000 souls were saved (Acts 2:41, Hebrews 8:1-13). The Holy Spirit did not assist individuals in keeping the requirements of this Old Covenant.

Although the Old Covenant was with Israel alone, it is rich with many treasures and guidelines that are valuable for the Christian. The tabernacle, the feast days, the Ark of the Covenant, mercy seat, and tabernacle items were all shadows and types of Jesus that are fulfilled in the New Testament. Much of the Old Testament instructions, concepts and precepts hold their value beyond the cross and the Christian can benefit greatly by the guidance they provide. It is foolish, however, to hold on to the shadows and types, and to incorporate them into our worship and Christian activities, when the type and shadows have become substance through the finished work of Jesus.

The New Covenant of grace. (Promise)
- Hebrews 8:1-13

- It is similar to God's covenant with Abraham in that the only requirement is for the individual to believe in Jesus.

- It is a Covenant between the Father and the Son (Galatians 3:16, Hebrews 8:6, 12:24).

- A person is automatically included in this covenant at the moment of the new birth (1 Corinthians 12:13, Romans 6:3-8).

- It is a covenant of grace with Jesus as the provider (John 1:16-17). Moses represents the law and condemnation. Jesus represents acceptance and all the benefits of grace.

- It has replaced the obsolete Old Covenant (Hebrews 8:7-13).

- Under this covenant, the Holy Spirit provides believers with the grace to be the saints that God declares them to be and enables them to walk in righteousness (Acts 1:3-8, Acts 2:33).

- It provides believers with an inheritance as heirs and joint heirs with Christ (John 1:12, Romans 8:14-17).

- It supplies Christians with everything they need for life and godliness (2 Peter 1:3).

- It imputes righteousness to the believer as a gift not as a performance (2 Corinthians 5:21, Romans 5:17).

- It frees from all condemnation of the Law (Romans 8:1-4).

- It liberates believers from the punishment and power of sin (Romans 6:14, 1 Corinthians 6:11, Hebrews 10:17).

- It declares believers to be saints rather than sinners (1 Corinthians 1:2, Hebrews 10:10, 14).

- It makes all the promises in Jesus "yes" (2 Corinthians 1:20).

- It provides Christians with eternal security through the sealing of the Holy Spirit (1 Corinthians 1:22, Ephesians 4:30).

- It is a covenant with blessings only and no curses (Galatians 3:13).

- It is superior to the law in that it provides life not death, praise not condemnation.

- It is absolute not conditional

- It is spiritual not carnal

- It is universal not local

- It is eternal not temporal.

- It is individual not national

- It is internal not external

- It has better promises and they are all yes!

- Hebrews 8:1-2,6 (1) Now this is the main point of the things we are saying; we have such a High Priest who is seated at the right hand of the throne of the Majesty in the heavens

(2) A minister of the sanctuary and of the true tabernacle which the Lord erected and not man.

(6) But now He has obtained a more excellent ministry, inasmuch as He is also Mediator of a better covenant which was established on better promises. (Hebrews 8:1-2, 6)

God designed the New Covenant of grace to satisfy all the Christian needs to live and enjoy a productive life in the Kingdom of God.

Chapter Five

Rightly Dividing the Word of God

The true Church is the beloved bride of Christ and is an essential element in the Kingdom of God. It is through the local assemblies of the Church that the Holy Spirit gives revelation and guidance for Kingdom principles. The Church has the responsibility to guide its members through all stages of maturation. It does this through encouraging, equipping, teaching and demonstrating the many actions and attitudes of the Kingdom. The Church holds the mirror of God's word before its members so that they are always presented with the true picture of who God declares them to be.

However, many modern churches have unintentionally-in most cases-taught their congregations doctrinal beliefs that are contrary to the New Covenant of grace. Many of these beliefs are the result of trickle down theology formulated in denominational seminaries. This theology consists of teachings that require the Christian to follow laws established under the Mosaic covenant and/or teachings that include a mixture of law and grace. Although it acknowledges that a person is saved by the grace of God alone, it maintains there are certain requirements and restrictions one must follow in order to sustain a right standing with God and with the church. Most of these teachings contain some form of sin management such as a continuous confession of sins-sins that must be confessed to retain one's righteousness.

Others teach that major portions of Paul's teaching regarding spiritual gifts passed away with the canonization of the Bible. This theology has greatly impacted how the Christian perceives and responds to God and to others. As they attempt to govern their lives and activities based upon these false teachings, they are destined to fail both internally and externally. They are in a losing battle of always trying to manage their lives so they will be free of sin. The result is that many live in bondage never enjoying the freedoms that Christ died to provide.

The true Church has been plagued with these teachings from the time of the transition from the Old Covenant of Law to the New Covenant of grace. The opposition to Paul's teaching of grace by the followers of Judaism, is basically the same opposition that has infiltrated the church from its founding to modern times.

Rightly interpreting scripture is fundamental to understanding its true meaning and application to the believer. Knowing the true application of the scriptures liberates us to enjoy the benefits of our relationship with our living Savior. There are a few simple rules that we can follow that assist us in determining the true meaning and application of a scripture. All scripture is given by inspiration of God but not all scripture is relevant for the Christian. Rightly dividing the word of truth implies individual study of the scriptures and the desire to know their content and context. In many cases, rightly dividing the word is simply discerning whether the scripture applied to the Old or New covenant.

- 2 Timothy 2:15 – Be diligent to present yourself approved to God, a worker who does not need to be ashamed, <u>rightly dividing the word of truth</u>. (Emphasis mine)

- 2 Timothy 3:16 –All scripture is given by inspiration of God, and is profitable for doctrine, for reproof, for correction, for instruction in righteousness. (All scripture is profitable for the purpose it was given but not all scripture applies to Christians.)

The cross stands as the separating line between the Old and New Covenants because it represents the finished work of Jesus' redemption of mankind. In our studies of the scriptures, it is important to realize that the writings of Matthew, Mark, Luke and John chronicled the life and times of Jesus while under the Old Testament (Covenant) and the New Testament (Covenant) did not actually begin until the death, burial and resurrection of Christ had occurred. After His resurrection Jesus instructed His disciples to wait in Jerusalem until the promised coming of the Holy Spirit. This actually took place on Pentecost fifty days after Jesus' death on the day of Passover. With the coming of the Holy Spirit the New Covenant was made available to all who would believe in Jesus. This was also the beginning of the Church age. As evidence of the empowerment of the Holy Spirit the new believers all spoke in tongues and three thousand souls were saved. The Holy Spirit's ministry is to give new birth, baptize into the body of Christ, seal and empower the believer with the grace necessary for them to develop as a child of Christ and be His representative to a lost world.

Christians are under the New Covenant of grace and free from the requirements of the Old Covenant of Law. Since the cross is the dividing line between the covenants, scripture must be examined as to its application under the New Covenant. There are many scriptures that applied to the laws under the Old Covenant that were terminated at the cross. An obvious example is animal sacrifice for the covering of sin. It stopped at the cross because Jesus made the ultimate sacrifice, therefore eliminating the need for further animal sacrifice. Many other requirements such as dietary restrictions, temple practices, and priestly duties were also terminated and made obsolete by the New Covenant. Jesus fulfilled the requirements of the Law. Therefore, to saddle the Christian church with such things is not only unnecessary, but outright wrong.

The nature of other Old Covenant laws and principles were changed at the cross. The Sabbath rest under the Old Covenant was a rest from all labor for Israelites and servants. Under the New Covenant the Sabbath rest becomes a rest in the finished work of Jesus Christ, freeing the Christian from struggling with the activities and issues that Jesus has already provided. Worship on the Sabbath (seventh) day was expanded to worship on any day. Most Christians choose to worship on the first day of the week, but regardless of the day chosen, the principle of giving God first place in our worship remains.

Many of the truths of the Old Testament remain valid and valuable on either side of the cross. In Proverbs a person is cautioned to "Keep his heart with all diligence for out of it spring the issues of life" (Proverbs 4:23). Jesus taught that it was out of the abundance of the heart that the mouth speaks. Under the New Covenant we are encouraged to have the mind of Christ, to guard our tongue, and to renew our mind to the principles and attitudes of the gospel of grace.

A valid way of examining the scriptures is to approach them with the following questions:

- <u>To whom was it written</u>? God spoke specific directions to Old Testament believers such as Abraham, Moses, the Prophets, and Israel. He also gives specific guidelines for Christians. Therefore, what is its context? How does it relate to the verses before and after? How does it relate to other scriptures concerning the same topic? The Scriptures themselves are the best commentary on their true meaning because all scripture relating to a particular topic or subject will be harmonious.

- <u>What does it say</u>? What is its content? What is its true meaning? It is important for us to determine what God meant the scripture to mean not the interpretation of others.

- <u>How does it apply to the Christian in the light of:</u>

- Covenant. Is it an application for Old Testament individuals or does it apply under the New Covenant?

- The finished work of Jesus Christ. Does it require one to do something that Christ has already accredited to him?

- Performing certain activities to be accepted by God?

- Having to follow certain rules and restrictions in order to maintain our righteousness or our relationship with God. Actions such as confessing all my sins, tithing, church attendance, not drinking alcohol, and involvement in non-Christian activities.

- Does it require me to forgive others or confess my sins in order for me to be forgiven?

Using these guidelines let us examine the following verses of scriptures:

1. Matthew 6:14 –15 – "For if you forgive men their trespasses, your heavenly Father will also forgive you. 15- But if you do not forgive men their trespasses, neither will your Father forgive your trespasses".

- Who was it spoken to? What is its context? (Matthew 4:25 and 7:28-29) reveals that Jesus was speaking to the multitudes that followed Him. These followers were still under the Old Covenant Law. They were accustomed to being taught by the scribes. Jesus was refining the requirements of the law.

- What is it saying (content)? It is saying very clearly that if a person does not forgive others then God will not forgive him.

- How does it apply to Christians in the light of the New Covenant and other scriptures on forgiveness? The scriptures state emphatically that all sin was forgiven through the sacrifice of Jesus on the cross. Jesus endured the wrath of God against all sin so that the world could be forgiven. Therefore, these verses do not apply to those under the New Covenant who are already forgiven of all sin and are already the righteousness of God. The Christian's forgiveness is not based upon whether he confesses his sin or forgives others. It is totally based upon what Jesus accomplished on the cross when He said, "it is finished".

To insist that these scriptures apply to the believer then one must also embrace the teaching that if your eye causes you to sin it should be plucked out and cast from you, and if your hand causes you to sin it should also be cut off and cast from you as a reminder that your sin will cause you to go to Hell. However, the scriptures state very clearly that both sin (noun) and sin (verb) are already forgiven and do not prevent us from entering Heaven. The only sin that causes a person to be cast into Hell is the sin of unbelief (Matthew 5:29-30, John 16:9).

To argue that these scriptures apply to the believer is to invalidate the finished work of Jesus on the cross. To claim that we must forgive before we can be forgiven by God is to imply that the sacrifice of Jesus was not sufficient.

To believe that we are totally forgiven because of our belief in Christ in no way lessens the importance of forgiveness. Forgiveness is a virtue that expresses the love of God. We do not forgive so that we may be forgiven; we forgive because we are forgiven (Ephesians 4:32, Colossians 3:13). It is paramount for the Christian to always maintain an attitude of forgiveness toward others because:

- It heals

- It restores relationships

- It acknowledges our wrongs

2. 1 John 1:9 – If we confess our sins, He is faithful and just to forgive us our sins and to cleanse us from all unrighteousness.

- To whom was it written and what is its context? Just a casual study of First John will reveal that in the first chapter John was addressing the Gnostics of that day and their intellectual false beliefs. False teachers had invaded the church and John wrote to refute them. There are no verses in the writings of Paul, Peter, or

36

John that require a Christian to confess their sins in order for God to forgive them. The only verse that encourages Christians to confess their sins is one that says to confess sins to one another, thereby maintaining a transparency in relationships. If this verse in First John is taken to apply to the Christian, then it is totally out of context with all the scriptures that declare we are already forgiven. Clearly, the meaning is for those that are still lost.

- What does it say? If a person sins he must confess that sin before he can be forgiven. It further indicates that when a person sins he becomes unrighteous and remains unrighteous until he confesses his sin.

- How does it apply under the New Covenant in light of other scriptures? The verse starts with a condition "if". Meaning if we confess our sins He will forgive us, which assumes that if we do not confess, He will not forgive. There are numerous problems associated with this verse if applied to the Christian. First, it implies that, in order to confess all sins, the person must be able to recall every sin. Otherwise, he would never be forgiven of those sins. Second, it implies that a person's sins make him unrighteous, otherwise there would be no need for the cleansing. This leads to the belief that one remains unrighteous until he/she confesses their sins, and then they become unrighteous again as soon as they sin again. Therefore, righteousness could never be a permanent state, only a temporary state in between a person's confession and his next sin. It implies that a person's performance dictates the level of his righteousness. Third, if we use this as the means for a Christian to remain righteous, we must in effect do away with all teachings that say Jesus died for all sins, for all people, for all time. Fourth, we must also reject the teachings that righteousness is a gift, and has nothing to do with how we perform. How can we be the righteousness of God and unrighteous at the same time? Fifth, God does not remember our sins and He does not hold sin against us. Therefore why would He still require us to confess them? Sixth, it was obvious that John was not speaking to redeemed individuals in chapter one, but was addressing the false beliefs of Gnosticism. He does not address them as "little children", until the second chapter. Seventh, the Gnostics do not have fellowship with God. They need to hear John's message of redemption. They walk in darkness. They need to be purified from sin. They still need to be purified from their unrighteousness.

There are no verses in the New Testament (Acts – Revelation) that require a Christian to confess his sins in order to be forgiven, that was a completed act on the cross. This does not devalue the true meaning of confession. We do not confess to get forgiven, we confess to acknowledge our wrong doing and make the necessary adjustments to amend our actions or attitudes. The Greek word for confess is "Homologeo" which means – Homo= the same, Logeo= to say, i.e. Thus confess means to say the same.

- We are encouraged to confess our sins one to another; to agree with each other concerning acts or attitudes of sin (James 5:16).

- Jesus is the High Priest of our confession (Hebrews 3:1). This means we should say the same thing that He says about all things. If it is wrong we say it is wrong and confess that wrong. If He says we are the righteousness of God we say we are the righteousness of God. As He is so are we in the world. (1 John 4:17)

3. <u>Galatians 5:4</u> – You have become estranged from Christ, you who attempt to be justified by law; you have fallen from grace.

- To whom was it written? It is written to the Christians at Galatia but it applies to all Christians.

- What does it say? It is clear here that Paul is not teaching that by falling from grace they lose their salvation. Beginning with verse one he is urging them to stand fast in the freedom that Christ had secured for them through grace and not go back under the bondage of the law. He warns them that since circumcision is a requirement of the Old Covenant if they submit to circumcision they are placing themselves back under the entirety of the old Law and in so doing reject all that Christ had obtained for them. They fall from grace to go back under the law.

- How does it apply under the New Covenant? It clearly teaches that once a person has been saved by grace and has access to all the benefits of the New Covenant, then decides to place himself back under some tenet of the old Law, he becomes obligated to keep all of the requirements of the Law. By attempting to be justified by keeping the Law, he forfeits the benefits of the New Covenant and makes what Christ has done of no value to him.

4. Matthew 6:33 – But seek first the kingdom of God and His righteousness and all these things shall be added to you.

- To whom was it spoken? It was spoken to the multitudes that followed Jesus, who were still under the Old Covenant encouraging them to seek the Kingdom that He was representing and the righteousness provided by that Kingdom. Although Christians are not seeking for the Kingdom to come, they are encouraged throughout the writings of Paul to seek the aspects of the Kingdom of which they are a part (Colossians 3:1, Romans 9:9-21).

- What is it saying? It was saying to Jew and Christian that everything they need and require is provided through the Kingdom of God.

- How does it apply under the New Covenant? It reminds Christians of the importance of keeping their focus on the Kingdom of God and His righteous way of living. Both His Kingdom and His righteousness are gifts to the Christian, but as children they must renew their mind to the ways of the Kingdom.

The following false statements are taught in various forms in many modern churches:

- We are just sinners saved by grace (meaning that our basic nature is to sin). By the grace of God, we have a new nature and are called saints. We may sin but we are saints and saints practice righteousness.

- We are saved to serve (meaning our highest calling is to give our lives to Christian ministry, in service for Jesus). Although Christians have many responsibilities, these are performed out of an intimate relationship with Christ. Not all Christians are called into Christian ministry but all are called to represent Him to a lost world.

- Christians should tithe at least ten percent of their income to the church. The requirement to tithe was an Old Covenant law for Old Covenant purposes. Under the New Covenant of grace, it is generous giving that is taught.

- We are saved by grace through faith but we must maintain our righteousness by following the guidelines for righteousness in the scriptures. According to the New Covenant scriptures we are made righteous through believing in Christ and not by works.

- We sin every day, either in word, action or thought. This teaching causes one to focus on sin management. The Bible teaches that we should be righteousness conscious and not sin conscious.

- When we sin against God, we are out of fellowship until we repent. Since all sin has been forgiven and God chooses not to remember it, sin does not prevent our fellowship with God.

- God will not hear our prayers if there is sin in our lives. God has settled the sin problem and welcomes our prayers as His children.

- We struggle with sin because of the old nature within us. Romans 6:6 declares that the old man (nature) died on the cross and we were given a new divine nature.

- We will give an account of our sins when we stand before the judgment seat of God. If this were true Jesus failed.

- Fasting, prayer and daily bible reading will make us better people. Nothing we can do will make us more righteous than what God declares us to already be. However, these things will certainly benefit us in many ways.

God anticipated everything that a believer would need to live a victorious life as a productive member of His Kingdom and made all those things available through the death and resurrection of Jesus His Son. He has given us everything that pertains to life and godliness. All His promises to us are "yes". He loves us and desires us to be successful, happy and prosperous. He has given us the written word to instruct us regarding our relationship to Him and His love and mercy toward us. We are privileged to study and discover the nuggets of truth that He has left us in His word.

Chapter Six

Living in Grace

I read the following story written by an unknown author during one of my studies and realized that it expressed how we often approach our daily activities with a mindset of what we must do to please God.

The story: A typical day in the life of Jesus: Jesus awakens in the guest room of Martha, Mary and Lazarus. It is a beautiful morning, and He hears the birds singing outside and smells the delicious breakfast that Martha is preparing. He dresses and puts on His sandals and begins to think about His day. His first thoughts are that He would like to take a day off and just spend time with His three friends. But then He realizes that He has many things to do that day for the Father. He will be going to Capernaum where He will be preaching to a large crowd. That will please the Father, and there will be many there that need various types of healing. The Father will be pleased to see them made well. There are also those that are oppressed by evil spirits and the Father will be pleased to see them set free. So He steps out on His day to accomplish these things for the Father.

We might think that this sounds like what a typical day in the life of Jesus would be like. The truth however, is that Jesus never began His day thinking of the great things He would do for God. We know this because He said so on several occasions. Jesus' earthly ministry was to reveal what the Father was like and to model the Kingdom of God. To accomplish this He put aside his deity and lived on earth as a normal man. He yielded his life to the life of God in him and allowed the Father to direct all His efforts and activities.

- John 5:19 – Then Jesus answered and said to them, "Most assuredly, I say to you, the Son can do nothing of Himself, but what He sees the father do; for whatever He does, the Son also does in like manner".

- John 5:30 – I can of Myself do nothing. As I hear, I judge, and My judgment is righteous, because I do not seek My own will but the will of the Father who sent me.

- John 7:16 – My doctrine is not Mine but His who sent Me.

- John 8:28 – Then Jesus said to them, "When you lift up the Son of Man, then you will know that I am He, and that I do nothing of Myself; but as My Father taught Me, I speak these things".

- John 8: 42 – If God were your Father, you would love Me, for I proceeded forth and came from God; nor have I come of Myself, but He sent me.

- John 12:49 –For I have not spoken on My own authority, but the Father who sent Me gave Me a command, what I should say and what I should speak.

- Acts 2:22 – Men of Israel, hear these words: Jesus of Nazareth, a Man attested by God to you by miracles, wonders, and signs which God did through Him in your midst, as you yourselves also know.

These verses reveal the mindset of Jesus was to do only what the Father directed Him to do and in doing so He could accurately present to the world what God the Father was like. Jesus never set out on His daily activities to accomplish tasks that He believed would please the Father. Jesus demonstrated what a normal person was capable of doing under the direction of the Holy Spirit. Why is this important? If Jesus had accomplished all that He did as God, then we would know it would be impossible for us to accomplish the same things. Yet, He said we would do greater things.

However, contrary to the way Jesus approached every day, we begin our days with unwritten lists of things that we feel we must accomplish for God. These are mental lists that we have accumulated through years of false teaching. We believe there are things we must do and ways we must act to please God. We are driven by what we think we must accomplish, while at the same time defeating all manner of sinful thoughts and actions; all to be accepted by Him. We have been exposed to this type of thinking from the time we were children. When things do not go well, we assume that we have committed some sin or wrong and need to confess, but when things are going well we assume that God is pleased with us. The truth is that our performance has nothing to do with God being pleased with us. That is settled in our position in Christ. The fact is that Jesus never expects us to do good things to be accepted by Him.

The Holy Spirit does not empower us so we can keep from sinning. He empowers us to live righteously. Jesus took care of our sin problem. The Holy Spirit's ministry is to enable us to become the people God designed us to be and to accomplish our responsibility as children of God. As we allow Him to direct our lives, our daily activities, we will accomplish all that He desires us to do without the strain, effort and worry often associated with living the good Christian life.

We are not called to live by principles or to live for Jesus. We may have been taught we are to live by biblical principles and although this sounds spiritual, it is just a subtle form of legalism, making principles a type of law. There are instructions in the Bible about how we should live and conduct our lives. However, these instructions are not religious laws for us to follow. They are descriptions of the many ways that Christ can live His life through us as we depend upon Him. The New Covenant is not grounded in what we must do but in what Jesus has already done.

- 1 Thessalonians 5:24 – He who calls you is faithful who also will do it.

- Philippians 1:6 – being confident of this very thing, that He who has begun a good work in you will complete it until the day of Jesus Christ.

- The Holy Spirit is also the Kingdom of God. He establishes His kingdom within us and releases the activities of the kingdom in and through us.

- Romans 14:17 – for the kingdom of God is not eating and drinking, but <u>righteousness</u>, and <u>peace</u> and <u>joy</u> IN THE HOLY SPIRIT. (Emphasis mine)

- Matthew 6:31 – Therefore do not worry, saying, "What shall we eat? Or what shall we drink? Or what shall we wear?"

- Matthew 6:32 – for after all these things the Gentiles seek. For your heavenly Father know that you need all these things.

- Matthew 6:33 – But seek first the kingdom of God and His righteousness, and all these things shall be added to you."

- John 15:5 – I am the vine, you are the branches. He who abides in Me, and I in him, bears much fruit; for without Me you can do nothing.

Think of our sphere of activity, responsibility, and influence as an active cell in the life of the body. Think of this sphere as having the life of God flowing into it, furnishing it with everything required for a healthy life. This is our life in Christ. Jesus is the personification of grace. He is the grace life and as we allow Him to direct our lives and activities, He accomplishes through us all that is required of us.

We are more productive and successful as we approach our Christian responsibilities from a position of resting in Christ and what He has done. Hebrews Chapter four speaks of such a rest.

- Hebrews 4:1 – Therefore, since a promise remains of entering His rest, let us fear lest any of you seem to have come short of it.

- Hebrews 4:2 – for indeed the gospel was preached to us as well as to them; but the word which they heard did not profit them, not being mixed with faith in those who heard it.

- Hebrews 4:3 – for we who have believed do enter that rest, as He has said. "So I swore in My wrath they shall not enter My rest."

In six days God spoke the universe into being, created the earth, all animal life, and all vegetation and set in perpetual motion all that we see today. Then the Bible says that He rested. Why? He had created and established a physical world for men to abide in and rule over and had established the perimeters of man's redemption.

Then we fast forward to the last Passover and to a cross on Golgotha's hill. Jesus is calling out, "My God, My God why have You forsaken Me." He has no sense of the Father's presence because all the sins of all time have been placed upon Him. He is suffering as a murderer, as a rapist, as a liar, as a blasphemer, as a terrorist, as the vilest of all sinners. The wrath of God is being poured out on Him for the punishment of all the sins of all the people for all times.

Finally God's wrath is satisfied. God is no longer angry toward people who sin. Forgiveness now flows from the heart of God toward all who have sinned. He has no more condemnation for them but only an unconditional love for mankind. Then Jesus speaks and says, "It is finished." He bows His head and gives up His Spirit. No one took His life; He gave it up for us.

After three days in the grave Jesus was resurrected and ascended to the Tabernacle in Heaven not made with hands. If this tabernacle was not made with hands, it must have been spoken into existence. This is the tabernacle that was used as the model given to Moses for earthly tabernacles. Jesus entered the tabernacle to perform His priestly rites as the High Priest after the order of Melchizedek. When He had finished His priestly duties, He sat down at the right hand of the Father because the entire plan for the salvation of man was finished, completed. There was nothing else to be done. He had done it all. And He rested.

These things were written that we may have a record showing everything required for our salvation has already been done. We can rest in that fact. We are assured that He will not condemn us, nor punish us and that He loves us unconditionally. He has deposited to our account all that Jesus secured for us. It is our inheritance. He wants us to rest in these facts and not believe that we must be doing something for Him to please Him. All we are required to do is believe this and allow His life to accomplish, in and through us, all that He desires for us. What a marvelous gift from God.

- Matthew 11:28- Come to Me, all you who labor and are heavy laden, and I will give you rest.

- Matthew 11:29 – Take My yoke upon you and learn from Me, for I am gentle and lowly in heart, and you will find rest in your souls.

- Matthew 11:30 – For My yoke is easy and My burden is light.

How can we know if we are resting?

- John 14:26 – But the Helper, the Holy Spirit, whom the Father will send in My name, He will teach all things, and bring to your remembrance all things that I said to you.

- John 14:27 – Peace I leave with you, My peace I give to you; not as the world gives do I give to you. Let not your heart be troubled, neither let it be afraid.

The two indicators that we are not resting in Christ are that our heart is troubled, and that we are afraid. We often say that we can do nothing apart from Christ. While this is a true statement, it also may hinder us from attempting great things. The better view would be to say, "I can do all things through Christ who strengthens me" (Philippians 4:13).

-   Philippians 1:6 – Being confident of this very thing, that He who has begun a good work in you will complete it until the day of Jesus Christ.

-   Philippians 2:13 – For it is God who works in you both to will and to do for His good pleasure.

-   Hebrews 13:21 –Make you complete in every good work to do His will, working in you what is well pleasing in His sight, through Jesus Christ, to whom be glory forever and ever, Amen".

Jesus is grace. His life flowing through us is the grace life. It will provide all that we need in our sphere and accomplishes all that is required of us.

Chapter Seven

Our Union in Christ

In his original state, Adam was a perfect, complete individual. God had designed him with a spirit, soul and physical body. God completed Adam by breathing life into him. Adam's mind was capable of receiving God's thoughts, and his will was free to choose his life activities. Adam's identity was in his relationship with God, and there was no knowledge or desire of any type of evil or sin. He and Eve had no conscious sense of wrong in their nakedness and were totally free in all their thoughts and actions. In this state of innocence, God gave Adam and Eve free access to all things on the earth, with one exception. They were not to eat of the tree of the knowledge of good and evil because to do so would cause their death. God's desire was not to restrict them but to protect them.

In their original state in the garden there was no good or evil. There was just the God life. The knowledge of good contained in the fruit of the tree of the knowledge of good and evil was itself evil because it was not something that God allowed for them. It is a form of goodness and self-righteousness that is developed or fashioned by the human mind without input from God. We see the evidence of this type of goodness demonstrated immediately after they ate of the fruit. Their first response was to see themselves naked and judged that to be evil. Then they attempted by self-effort to fix this by covering themselves with fig leaves. Now, instead of having the covering of God's glory, they attempt to cover themselves by means they determine to be good. This is the root of all religions, trying to cover sin by self-effort of self-righteous means.

In the New Testament when Jesus came to a fig tree covered with leaves, but had no fruit, He cursed it because it appeared to be something that it was not, fruitful. This represents man-made religions that also have an appearance of fruitfulness but bearing no real fruit.

These two trees in the garden are symbolic of the choices that we are faced with every day. Do we wish to obey God or do things our way? The tree of life is symbolic of grace, while the tree of the knowledge of good and evil represents the law. One leads to life eternal and the other to death. One is to trust and rely upon God and His directions for our lives, and the other is a trust in ourselves or others.

Adam was influenced by Eve to believe the lie of the devil that they could be more like God by eating of the tree of the knowledge of good and evil. Adam had no predisposition toward sin. So perhaps his motive was a desire to be more like God, not realizing that in his current state he was exactly that. The deception here is the idea that man can do something to make himself more like God. This deception is still one of the devil's weapons used against mankind. Adam and Eve had their identity in their relationship with God, but when they chose to believe the devil, their identity was derived from what they could acquire (the knowledge of good and evil).

In any event, when Adam and Eve ate of the fruit several things happened which they had never experienced. God had warned that if they ate of this fruit they would die. There was something inherent in the fruit of the knowledge of good and evil that brought death. As soon as they ate of the fruit their spirit died and death entered into their flesh. They began to die physically. When they rejected the God life and chose the knowledge of good and evil, they became separated from the source of true life and therefore were spiritually dead.

Now, there were other forces working within them, enticing them to do things that they had never even thought of and to find their identity in what they themselves could do. They genetically passed these entities to all mankind. Every human, with the exception of Jesus, was born with these two entities, the "flesh" and "sin principle".

In addition to death, two other sinister things happened because they had eaten of the fruit of the knowledge of good and evil. Their bodies were invaded by these two other sources: First there was an entity called the "flesh". The "flesh" represents all actions, attitudes and thoughts to establish identity, righteousness, approval, success, and security based upon conclusions of what is right or desired, without an input from the Holy Spirit. The flesh is comprised of a subconscious and conscious disposition. The subconscious portion is that portion that contains our basic drives that seek fulfillment and a desire to avoid pain or unpleasant things. It contains everything that is inherited and those things learned through the five senses that subconsciously influence our decisions. The conscious portion is that organized portion of our personality that includes all the mechanisms we use to establish our identity and acceptance. It includes defense mechanisms, accumulated intellectual knowledge, learned behavior, and acquired beliefs. It is what we call reason or common sense.

Many have been taught that they have two natures, a divine nature and a sinful nature, to explain the cause of the struggles within them. They have been told that it is like having a black dog and a white dog within them, and the one they feed the most will be the most powerful. While there is truth in that illustration regarding the spirit man and the flesh, it is untruthful in its design to prove we have two natures. The scriptures are clear that at the moment we accepted Christ our old self (nature) died, and we were born anew. We received a divine God nature. The Bible goes so far as to tell us that God's seed is within us. We have His DNA. God cannot and does not birth unholy children. Nature is defined as the inherent character or basic constitution of a person or thing. The concept of two natures even fails in the natural realm. God created everything "according to its kind" and it reproduces according to its kind. The truth is, in Christ we are a new person. The old man has died and we are born again with a new nature.

Our struggle as Christians is not against our old nature but against something the scriptures identify as the *flesh*. The *flesh* wishes to provide a sense of identity rooted in intellectual attributes, physical characteristics or social status. The *flesh* gains its identity from the soul (mind or intellect) or the body (family lineage or physical appearance) as opposed to the *spirit* – our new identity in Christ. Confidence in the flesh is a choice. We can choose to build our identity around our birth into a certain family, our associations, or our accomplishments (see Phil 3:4-6 where Paul talks about putting confidence in the flesh).

When we think of the *flesh* we normally think of such deeds as gossiping, lusting and other ugly manifestations of sin. Although these are certainly manifested by the flesh, the flesh is equally satisfied to initiate religious or moral living admired by others. The flesh will build any kind of identity as long as it gains love, attention, and acceptance from others. Paul asks the Galatians "Are you so foolish? Having begun in the Spirit, are you now being made <u>perfect by the flesh?</u>" (Gal 3:3) Here, the flesh was not trying to produce evil behavior in the Galatians. Instead, these Christians were using fleshly effort as a means of perfecting themselves in Christ. They considered their intellectual and moral beliefs as the way to spiritual maturity. A *flesh* -based method of self-improvement may appeal to us if we are not informed about God's way to maturity. God's way is simple: Jesus plus nothing.

Other Bible passages identify the flesh as"

- A way to think
- A way to walk
- Works against the Spirit
- Encourages self-effort
- Seeks identity and purpose

But the *flesh* is not the old self or a sinful nature. It is something within us, but it is not us. Before we were in Christ we had no choice and during that time through our physical senses we developed wrong beliefs, strong desires and defense mechanisms that helped form our identify and self-worth. This part of us was not converted when we were born again and so they still tempt us wrongly. The flesh is to the spirit as a spoiled rebellious child that needs to be constrained.

The second entity is called Sin or the "sin principle". Here Sin is a noun that identifies an evil influence within us that tempts us with evil thoughts and acts that are prohibited by God and society. This evil entity will not abide by the laws of God or man. When left to run rampant, it will father all kinds of horrendous acts and deeds. This evil force will disguise itself as being righteous in order to achieve a sinful goal. Paul refers to this entity in Romans chapter seven. Paul writes that apart from the law, "sin" is dead, but this insubordinate entity tempts us to abide by some portion of the law and therefore makes sin alive in us.

In the first reference to sin, God is speaking to Cain regarding his offering, "If you do well, will you not be accepted? And if you do not do well, sin lies at the door. And its desire is for you, but you should rule over it (Genesis 4:7). Cain in response to his flesh was attempting to be accepted by his own means. The word "lies" here means to crouch on all fours as a lion preparing to leap (1 Peter 5:8). God identifies this power that desires to rule over Cain as Sin. He was not speaking of specific acts of sin but an influencing power. God does not warn Cain about sinful behavior. Instead, He was concerned about an organized force complete with desires and an agenda to control. It is evident that this power came about as the result of the fall. If we can understand that this power exists, it will radically change the way that we think. A person-like power called sin was at work in Paul causing him to do things that he didn't intend to do. Paul says that this force was not him; it was something other than him, although it was acting through his physical body.

- Romans 7:17-21: -"But now, it is no longer I who do it, but sin that dwells in me. For I know that in me (that is, in my flesh) nothing good dwells; for to will is present with me, but how to perform what is good I do not find. For the good that I will to do, I do not do; but the evil I will not to do, that I practice. Now if I do what I will not to do, <u>it is no longer I</u> who do it, <u>but sin</u> that dwells in me. I find then a law, that evil is present with me, the one who wills to do good". (Emphasis mine)

Notice that Paul places the blame on something that was not him. Here we see that sinful thoughts were served up from a secondary source called sin. Sin lived in Paul, but sin was not Paul. The point is that there is a sin principle within the physical body and this sin principle is aroused when we try to live up to the law or any law-like standard. That principle is stirred up and empowered by the law.

- 1 Corinthians 15:56: - The sting of death is sin, (not sins) and the strength of sin is the law.

- Romans 4:15 - Because the law brings about wrath; for where there is no law there is no transgression.

- Romans 6:12: - Therefore do not let sin (not sins) reign in your mortal body, that you should obey it in its lusts (We give into sin by obeying its thoughts and desires.). (Emphasis mine)

- Phil. 4:8 -Finally, brethren, whatever things are true, whatever things are noble, whatever things are just, whatever things are pure, whatever things are lovely, whatever things are of good report, if there is any virtue and if there is anything praiseworthy – meditate on these things.

Think of the sin principle as a parasite that has invaded your body that causes damage and hurt. It is in you but it is not you. Yet, you suffer the effects of its presence in you. When our mind receives messages from this source of sin, these messages may feel or sound just like us – especially if we are not aware that our old self is dead and gone, and that our spirit man does not desire to sin. If we are unaware of who we really are, we may think that these messages originate with us. Not only will sin give you a wrong thought, but it will condemn you for having the wrong thought. A simple truth is that in Christ we have a new divine nature and that divine nature does not have evil and wrong thoughts. These thoughts can come from three places, the flesh, the sin principle, or the devil.

In the Old Testament circumcision was a sign of a seal of righteousness by faith for Abraham, and a sign of covenant for those under the Law. In the New Testament, baptism is the sign of righteousness for the Christian. The moment that we receive Christ as Savior the Holy Spirit baptizes us into Jesus. This is a spiritual baptism of which water baptism is a symbol. When He was crucified, we were crucified. When He died, we died, when He left the body of sin behind, we, through spiritual circumcision, were separated from our body of sin. When He arose, we arose. This provides us with power over the "flesh" and the "sin principle" which are still at work in our bodies. This is referred to as "circumcision made without hands" because it is likened to the Old Covenant procedure of circumcision where a part of the skin is taken off and is no longer a part of the person. In this spiritual circumcision, the flesh and sin principle are no longer a part of the true person who is sealed in Christ. This is why Paul could say in Romans Chapter seven that "it" (sin) was not him.

Paul writes again in Romans eight that the bodies of those in Christ were dead, but the Spirit was the true life. In this process our spirit is placed into His Spirit, but our bodies are not placed in Him. Our true identity is in this spiritual union and is not to be identified with the works of the flesh. The flesh is sentenced to die. It cannot be saved nor can it be sanctified. Our fleshy bodies will all die eventually because the sentence of death that was passed upon Adam was passed down on all flesh. Our bodies bear the characteristics of death (aging, loss of sight, loss of hearing, etc), not life, just as the characteristics of cancer are death and can under no circumstance ever produce life. The flesh and sin principle entered Adam's body in the similar manner in which cancer invades the body, and just like cancer, they brought about death to his physical body. Our human body is an earth suit, but it is not us any more than a space suit is the astronaut that wears it. One day we will shed these earth suits and receive a glorified body fashioned after God's original design.

The segment of our minds that has not been renewed to grace thinking will agree and cooperate with the Law, flesh and sin. But we have received the divine seed (DNA) of God and our spirit has been sealed by the Holy Spirit and cannot sin. When we are born spiritually we are perfect and complete in Christ, but we are not complete in our knowledge of who we are and must progressively learn who we are and live in that knowledge. Our mind must be renewed to have the mind of Christ because that portion of the mind that is not renewed will agree and support the desires of our flesh.

Even though the Holy Spirit makes our body His temple, our body is not in Him. In like manner, we live in Him but our body is not in Him. We must understand that the flesh is not us and that God does not condemn us for the sins of the flesh. It is also important for us to understand that our body was neither sanctified nor saved. Therefore, we are still subject to its influences and temptations.

Are there consequences to sins of the flesh? Certainly there are consequences, and some of these are grave consequences. I am accountable for those sins of the flesh that I allow because of the effects upon others and myself. Some of the consequences include damaged relationships, hurts, sickness, causing others to sin, confusion in others, damage to one's body, and a host of other things. For the Christian, all sin comes from a rejection of grace in some manner.

Reference:
- Romans 5:12 – Therefore, just as through one man sin entered the world, and death through sin, and thus death spread to all men, because all sinned.

- Galatians 2:20 – I have been crucified with Christ; it is no longer I who live, but Christ lives in me; and the life which I now live in the flesh I live by faith in the Son of God, who loved me and gave Himself for me.

- Romans 6:6 – Knowing this, that our old man was crucified with Him, that the body of sin might be done away with, that we should no longer be slaves of sin.

- Galatians 5:24 – And those who are Christ's have crucified the flesh with its passions and desires.

- Ephesians 2:15 – Having abolished in His flesh the enmity, that is the law of commandments contained in ordinances, so as to create in Himself one new man from the two, thus making peace.

- Romans 8:10 –"and if Christ is in you, the <u>body is dead because of sin</u>, but the Spirit is life because of righteousness." (Emphasis mine)

- Romans 7:8 – But sin, taking opportunity by the commandment, produced in me all manner of evil desire. For apart from the law sin was dead.

- Romans 7:17 – But now, it is no longer I who do it, <u>but sin that dwells in me</u>. (Emphasis mine)

- Romans 7:18 – For I know that in me (that is, in my flesh) nothing good dwells; for to will is present with me, but how to perform what is good I do not find

- Romans 7:24 – O wretched man that I am! Who will deliver me from this body of death?

- Romans 7:25 – I thank God – through Jesus Christ our Lord! So then, with the mind I myself serve the law of God, but with the flesh the law of sin.

- Romans 3:20 –Therefore by the deeds of the law no flesh will be justified in His sight, for by the law is the knowledge of sin.

- Romans 8:8 – So then, those who are in the flesh cannot please God.

- Romans 4:11 – And he received the sign of circumcision, a seal of the righteousness of the faith which he had while still uncircumcised, that he might be the father of all those who believe, though they are uncircumcised, that righteousness might be imputed to them also.

- John 3:3- Jesus answered and said to him, "Most assuredly, I say to you, unless one is born again, he cannot see the kingdom of God.

- John 3:5 – Jesus answered, "Most assuredly, I say to you, unless one is born of water and the Spirit, he cannot enter the kingdom of God

- John 3:6 -That which is born of the flesh is flesh, and that which is born of the Spirit is spirit.

- Corinthians 15:50 – Now this I say, brethren, that flesh and blood cannot inherit the kingdom of God; nor does corruption inherit incorruption.

- 1 Corinthians 15:56 –The sting of death is sin, and the strength of sin is the law.

- Colossians 2:11 – In Him you were also circumcised with the circumcision made without hands, by putting off the body of the sins of the flesh, by the circumcision of Christ. (Emphasis mine)

- Colossians 2:12 –Buried with Him in baptism, in which you also were raised with Him through faith in the working of God, who raised Him from the dead.

- Colossians 2:13 – And you, being dead in your trespasses and the uncircumcision of your flesh, He has made alive together with Him, having forgiven you all trespasses.

- Colossians 2:14 – Having wiped out the handwriting of requirements that was against us, which was contrary to us. And He has taken it out of the way, having nailed it to the cross.

- Colossians 2:15 – Having disarmed principalities and powers. He made a public spectacle of them, triumphing over them in it.

- 1 John 3:9 – Whoever has been born of God does not sin, for His seed remains in him; and he cannot sin, because he has been born of God. (Emphasis mine)

- 2 Corinthians 1: 13 – Who also has sealed us and given us the Spirit in our hearts as a guarantee, (Emphasis mine)

- Ephesians 1:13 – In Him you also trusted, after you heard the word of truth, the gospel of your salvation, in whom also, having believed, you were sealed with the Holy Spirit of promise.

- Ephesians 4:30 – And do not grieve the Holy Spirit of God, <u>by whom you were sealed for the day of redemption. (Emphasis mine)</u>

- Hebrews 9:9 – It was symbolic for the present time in which both gifts and sacrifices are offered which cannot make him who performed the service perfect in regard to the conscience

- Hebrews 9: 14 – How much more shall the blood of Christ, who through the eternal Spirit offered Himself without spot to God, <u>cleanse your conscience from dead works to serve the living God.</u> (Emphasis mine)

The following three chapters address areas where grace has been misrepresented.

Chapter Eight

Tithing or Stewardship

Many great men of God differ as to whether or not tithing is a New Covenant responsibility and offer both scripture and revelatory supports to their beliefs. Since many modern churches extract certain aspects and requirements of the old Law, and teach them to their congregations there is an urgent need for the individual to examine the scriptures for himself and to rightly divide their meaning. This is especially true when separating the teachings of the old and new covenants. For the gospel to remain the true gospel there can be no mixture of the Old Testament covenant of Law and the New Testament of grace. To do so is to pollute the gospel of grace and bring confusion in the church. My goal in regards to tithing is not to eliminate the purpose of Christian giving, but to elevate the greater privilege of stewardship and giving.

Many questions have arisen about the requirement of tithing in the New Testament. The following questions will give one a framework to secure their own conclusions regarding tithing. I will attempt to answer some in this chapter.

- Do the scriptures require a Christian to tithe beyond doubt?

- What was the purpose of the tithe?

- What does the tithe include? I.e. money, produce, livestock, etc.

- Is there any record of the requirement to tithe prior to Abraham tithing to Melchizedek?

- Although Abraham tithed to Melchizedek, is there any other reference that he ever tithed again (Genesis 14: 20)?

- Who was Melchizedek?

- What did Abraham tithe to Melchizedek?

- What was the purpose of Abraham's tithe?

- Did Abraham tithing to Melchizedek set precedence for us to tithe?

- If tithing was already a requirement prior to the law, why did Jacob bargain with God about giving a tenth if God would bless him in certain ways?

- Does the fact that Levi paid tithes to Melchizedek, while still in Abraham's loin, set a precedence to tithe in the New Testament?

- Was there a greater reason that Levi, who received tithes, also tithed to Melchizedek?

- Was the tithe to Melchizedek to a person or to an organization?

- Does the scripture in Hebrews chapter seven actually teach that Christians should tithe to the Church?

- The Book of Acts is a history of the beginning of the church. Is there any record in Acts that indicates the Christian should tithe?

- Did the leadership at Jerusalem, in their letter to the gentile churches, require them to tithe?

The following overview of giving in the scriptures, regarding tithing, is not exhaustive but hopefully will be helpful.

Genesis 4:2-7 –These verses record the first act of giving to God in the scriptures. This act of giving is identified as an offering not a tithe. It was not given to a high priest, tabernacle, temple, or church, it was given to God. If there was a requirement to tithe, Adam and Eve should have also been involved. This appears to be an act of worship through giving of one's substance, since there is no written record that this was a requirement by God. There was no designated amount required to be given by either Cain or Abel. God rejected Cain's offering because of the condition of his heart and not because of what he offered. Abel's offering was an acknowledgement of his love for God and the understanding of the goodness of God, but Cain grudgingly gave. Abel's attitude of worship should be the motivation for all our giving. It acknowledges that all things belong to God, and that He graciously shares them with those He loves.

- 1 John 3:12 – Not as Cain who was of the wicked one and murdered his brother and why did he murder him? Because his works were evil and his brother's righteous.

Abraham: Genesis 14:18-20, Hebrews 7:1-28

The tithe went to a person, the High Priest of God Most High. Melchizedek was not the high priest over a church, synagogue, temple or tabernacle, but was a high priest who represented God alone. This was an act of worship by Abraham, acknowledging that his victory was a blessing from God and the fulfillment of a covenant promise. There is no record in any of the scriptures that required Abraham to give a tithe. The tenth was given from the spoils of war as an offering, not a required tithe. It is assumed here that Abraham gave a tenth of the gold and silver, a tenth of the livestock, a tenth of all the spoils. (Numbers 31:25-54 direct how the spoils of war are to be distributed).

Melchizedek was one of the Old Testament appearances of Jesus. These are known as "theophanies". (Other appearances of Jesus in the Old Testament are found in Genesis 3:8, Genesis 12:7, Genesis 17:1, Genesis 18:1, Genesis 32:24-30, Exodus 3:2-6, Joshua 5:13-15, Daniel 3:35.) Following this encounter with Melchizedek, there is no record that Abraham ever gave a tenth again, although it is recorded that he prospered in many ways and established altars in the land. If one follows Abraham's example of tithing, then once he has given his initial tithe he has fulfilled the requirement. The reference to Abraham giving tithes to Melchizedek in the book of Hebrews does not set precedence for tithing but rather states the superiority of the priesthood of Jesus over those appointed under the Old Covenant. The theme of the entire book of Hebrews is the superiority of Jesus over all other priests. The word "therefore" in Hebrews 7:11 verifies that all that has been said before validates the superiority of Jesus' ministry as High Priest. The correct rendering of Hebrews 7:8 is, under the Old Covenant, men who receive tithes die, but there, many years prior to the institution of the mandatory tithe, Melchizedek, as the greater high priest, received tithes as proof that he lives. This reference in Hebrews is used to connect the priesthood of Jesus with the order of Melchizedek, declaring that Jesus, although not from the line of appointed priests, was a greater high priest than those of Aaron's linage. What is established in these verses is that the lesser gives to the greater. The reference to Levi paying tithes to Melchizedek is a proof text, that even those who received tithes under the dictates of the Law of Moses gave tithes to a greater priest while in the loins of Abraham. The lesser gives to the greater. It would follow that if this were precedence for tithing, the author would have included all of Jacob's sons. There is no record that Levi or any of the other sons of Jacob gave tithes prior to the giving of the law. There is no clear reference in these verses that establish tithing for those under the New Covenant.

Jacob: Genesis 28:10-22

Jacob deceived Isaac out of the birthright that belonged to Esau. He was blessed by Isaac and sent by him to Padan Aram, where he was to seek a wife. He stayed over night at Luz. During the night, the Lord appeared to him in a dream and identified Himself as the God of Abraham and Isaac and told him how He would bless him in the future. There were no conditions that Jacob must meet in order for God to bless him. God "said these are the things I will do for you". This was an extension of the covenant that God made with Abraham. When Jacob awakens, he realizes that this is a special place and renames it Bethel, or house of God. He then makes a vow, telling God that if He will bless him as He said, then God would be his God and he would give a tenth of all that God gave him. That has the sound of bartering with God. This is the first mention of tithing for two generations and obviously was made as a reference to what Jacob had been told about his grandfather giving a tenth to Melchizedek. If tithing was already a requirement, then to tell God if He would do certain things, he would tithe, seems to be a foolish statement on Jacob's part. This was obviously a time of worship for Jacob and the offer of the tenth was to come as an act of worship, acknowledging the greatness and goodness of God. God did not require Jacob to give a tenth, this was a voluntary act on Jacob's part. There is also no record that Jacob fulfilled this vow nor taught his children to tithe.

Moses:

God, through Moses established the Old Covenant with Israel. The requirement to tithe was a part of this covenant. Although the tithe was established on Mount Sinai, at the early part of Israel's wilderness journey, there is no record of them tithing until they came into the Promised Land forty years later. The tithe had several purposes. One of the major purposes was to provide for the Levites who were given the assigned duties of attending the care of the tabernacle and temple and to provide for Aaron's sons as priests. Other purposes were to provide for strangers, orphans, the poor, and widows. The tithe was mostly from the first fruits of the land and herds.

- Numbers 18:21-32 – Tithes for the Levites

- Leviticus 27:30-34 – Things included in the tithe.

- Deuteronomy 14:22-29 – God directs individuals to eat their tithe or sell the tithe for money and buy whatever their heart desires. The church certainly does not teach this.

- Deuteronomy 26:12-15 – Certain tithes were required every three years for the Levites, strangers, fatherless, and widows.

- Nehemiah 10:35-39 – Tithe requirements and use.

Pharisees: Matthew 23:23; Luke 11:42

Jesus rebukes the Pharisees for going to extremes in tithing but neglecting more important things. These texts cannot be used as justification for New Testament tithing because this requirement was under the Old Covenant. The New Testament of grace did not begin until after the death and resurrection of Jesus.

- Hebrews 8:6 – But now He has obtained a more excellent ministry, inasmuch as He is also Mediator of a better covenant, which was established on better promises.

- Hebrews 8:13 – In that He says, "A new covenant." He has made the first obsolete. Now what is becoming obsolete and growing old is ready to vanish away.

Jesus came to introduce and model the Kingdom of God. He accomplished this through His teachings and interaction with the needs of the multitudes. There is no record of Jesus tithing during His time on earth. If He had done so He would have violated the biblical teaching that the lesser gives to the greater as Abraham did to Melchizedek recorded in Hebrews Seven.

Gentile Churches:

The obvious omission of the requirement to tithe, in any of Paul's letters to the gentile churches he founded or ministered to, must bear some weight that tithing is not a New Covenant requirement. A group of Jews came down to Antioch and taught the new converts that they must be circumcised and keep the Law, but Paul and Barnabas disputed with these Jews, saying that they were not under the Law. The final outcome was to go to Jerusalem and meet with the apostles and elders for an answer to resolve the matter. After much discussion and debate, the conclusion was to send a letter to the gentile churches outlining the guidelines they were to observe. There is no mention of tithing in these requirements. If tithing was to be a requirement under the New Covenant, surely they would have mentioned it in the letter to guide gentile churches. (Acts 15:1-29)

Paul wrote two thirds of the New Testament and does not mention tithing as a requirement in any of his writings. The book of Acts contains the history of the early church but there is no mention that the early church was required to tithe. Peter wrote two books of the New Testament and does not mention tithing. John wrote four books of the New Testament and does not mention tithing.

To consider tithing a New Testament requirement may lead one to assume that, after God gets His tenth, the rest remains for the individual to use as he desires. This undermines the concept of stewardship. If we are required to be stewards over everything that God entrusts to us then how would giving a tenth prove anything?

Some teach that giving the tithe voluntarily is an expression that the person is acknowledging that all he has comes as blessings from God. However, any true believer willingly acknowledges that everything he has is a blessing from God (James 1:17). If we must tithe to acknowledge that all we have comes from God, it is still a requirement and a requirement is a law. This could lead one to believe that if he does not or cannot tithe he is failing to acknowledge that everything comes from God. This also implies that a person must do something to prove to God that he understands all blessings come from Him and invalidates all that Jesus purchased for us on the cross. If this were true, how many times must a person tithe to prove to God that he understands everything comes from Him?

Tithing is a stronghold that places Christians under the Law, from which the Church must liberate its members. Teaching that tithing is a requirement under the New Covenant causes confusion and heaps guilt and condemnation on many Christians and is contending that law giving is superior to grace giving. Some leaders fear if they do not stress tithing, their congregations will not give the necessary funds to support the staff and the church needs. Sermons that explain grace stewardship and grace giving would alleviate this fear.

The New Testament Christian is unique because he is born again and placed into Christ as a child of God. He becomes an heir and joint heir to all that belongs to Christ. He has the covenant promise that he has been given everything that pertains to life and godliness. Neither Abraham, Moses, nor any under the Old Testament held this position in Christ. If we are joint heirs with Jesus, why would He require us to give back to Him something that He has given us as heirs? Would a man with a joint bank account with his wife require her to withdraw money from the account each week and give it to him to prove that she loves and trusts him? In this modern time, we have narrowed tithing down to only money, but true tithing under the old Law required much more than money. We attribute this to the change in times but, actually, we are picking and choosing which part of the Law we want to impose. When did the transition take place from the tithe including many things to only one thing, money? How much of a person's money must he tithe? Does he tithe on the net or gross income? What about widows and poor on a low fixed income? Church records will show that very few people really tithe; they give varying amounts of their income. Is this a sin that is allowed in the church? It is abundantly clear that the modern church does not follow the Old Testament guidelines for the use of the tithe. When were the new guidelines adopted?

When Jesus declared in John 19:30 "it is finished", He was declaring that He had accomplished all that was required to be done for the salvation of mankind. If in fact, Jesus did all that was required to be done and we cannot add to nor take from it, it should be taken for granted that this includes tithing, since tithing is a "doing".

John writes "as He is, so are we in this world" (1John 4:17). If something does not apply to Jesus, it does not apply to us. When we were born again we were placed in Jesus and in the Father. Since we are in Christ, God sees us the same as Jesus. Our new spirit is exactly like Him. In our spirit we have everything that pertains to life and godliness. Since all these things are already ours, why would God then require us to tithe in order to show that we know that all things come from Him?

- 2 Corinthians 9:7 – So let each one give as he purposes in his heart, not grudgingly or of <u>necessity</u>: "for God loves a cheerful giver.

- 2 Corinthians 9:8 – And God is able to make all grace abound toward you, that you, always having all sufficiency in all things, may have abundance for every good work.

These scriptures tell us how and why we should give. We must give whatever we purpose in our hearts to give. This should be under the guidance of the Holy Spirit. We are not to give grudgingly or of necessity but to give cheerfully.

The reason we are able to do this is that God makes all grace abound toward us so that we may always have all sufficiency in everything and may have abundance for every good work.

- 2 Peter 1:3 – as His divine power has given to us all things that pertain to life and godliness.

- Philippians 4:19 – And my God shall supply all your needs according to His riches in glory by Christ Jesus.

God's plan for the redemption of mankind is clear in both the teaching of Jesus and in the Epistles. There is no doubt left as to what a person must do to be saved. If redemption were as vague as tithing it would cause many to oscillate in what they believe they must do to be saved.

Some final thoughts: If tithing was established before Abraham's time, when was it established and with whom? There is no mention in the covenant God made with Abraham that he should tithe, in fact he did not have to give anything. Some teach that, because Abraham tithed before the establishment of the Law, that this sets the precedence to tithe under the New Covenant. Abraham also sacrificed animals before the Law was given. Does that establish a priority under the New Covenant that we should continue to sacrifice? Prior to the Law, a man could have multiple wives; does that also carry over to the New Covenant? Under the New Covenant it is God doing the giving and man receiving.

My conclusions and conviction: I do not believe tithing is a New Covenant requirement. To make it so, for any reason, would be to make it a law. I do, however, believe that we are to be good stewards of all that God entrusts to us and give out of those resources as the Holy Spirit directs us. I further believe that giving is one of the characteristics of our love and devotion to God. When we use what God has given us to meet the needs of others we are responding in a manner of grace. I further believe that the scriptures teach that we should support those who have spiritual leadership over us. I also believe we should give for the upkeep of the local church facilities. I think that Christians should support those ministries that seek the advancement of the Kingdom of God's grace. This attitude of giving acknowledges that we are stewards of all that God has entrusted to us, and we give, as He directs, to where He directs. I submit that those with this attitude will give far more than the tenth. I have formed this conclusion from my studies of the scriptures and have no ill feeling toward those who have come to different conclusions.

2 Corinthians 9:10-11 - Now may He who supplies seed to the sower, and bread for food, supply and multiply the seed you have sown and increase the fruits of your righteousness.

11 - While you are enriched in everything for all liberality, which causes thanksgiving through us to God.

Chapter Nine

Predestination from a Grace Perspective

The purpose of this chapter is not to convince those who believe in Calvinistic predestination to change their doctrinal beliefs, but, to provide the grace alternative for those millions of others who believe that God is a loving, kind, forgiving and compassionate God. It is for those who believe that He is a God who has done everything possible to keep people from going to Hell; not a God that would predestine some to Hell and others to Heaven, but a God who so loved the lost of the world that He sent His Beloved Son to die on a cross so men could be forgiven their sin and have a relationship with Him. This is the God of grace of the Bible.

I do not in any way doubt or dismiss the sovereignty of God. I believe that salvation is totally God's plan, apart from anything that man can do to save himself. I embrace the idea that the wisdom and plan of God for mankind is so great and magnificent, that it can, and does, reconcile any perceived differences that men have between predestination and the will of man. I futher believe that the love of God for mankind motivated Him to predestine a plan that would include the redemption of all mankind and then so designed man that, even in his fallen state, he would be able to respond and participate in this plan of redemption. I also believe that God has always known who would respond with belief in His Son and be saved and who would reject His Son and be damned.

To appropriately understand the doctrine of predestination versus the will of man to choose or reject God one must embrace an accurate biblical understanding of the nature and grace of God. The premise taught by John Calvin and his followers states that God is sovereign and that man is totally depraved, that man is spiritually dead to God and has no desire or ability to seek God. So, therefore, the only way an individual can be saved is for God to choose to give him/her understanding of his/her lost condition and faith to respond to Him. Most theologians agree with the sovereignity of God and that salvation of mankind is totally God's idea and plan. However, Calvinists teach that since all mankind is in a totally depraved state, God is justified in allowing those in this state to remain in this state. He can, and does, choose certain ones for salvation, but does not choose others. In effect, in His sovereignty God predestines some to Heaven and the remainder go to Hell and He is justified in doing so because all fallen mankind deserves hell. The following is a summary of this belief:

Loraine Boettner, in his book "The Reformed Doctrine of Predestination" has this to say: The Reformed Faith has held to the existence of an eternal, divine decree which, antecedently to any difference or desert in men themselves separates the human race into two portions and ordains one to everlasting life and the other to everlasting death. So far as this decree relates to men, it designates the counsel of God concerning those who had a supremely favorable chance in Adam to earn salvation, but who lost that chance. As a result of the fall they are guilty and corrupted; their motives are wrong and they cannot work out their own salvation. They have forfeited all claim upon God's mercy, and might justly have been left to suffer the penalty of their disobedience as all of the fallen angels were left. But instead the elect members of this race are rescued from this state of guilt and sin and are brought into a state of blessedness and holiness. The non-elect are simply left in their previous state of ruin, and are condemned for their sins. They suffer no unmerited punishment, for God is dealing with them not merely as men but as sinners". This in a nutshell outlines the perimeters of Calvinism as voiced by those who assume they are the predestined elect and appointed by God to correct those who believe in the love and grace of a benevolent God.

Calvinism teaches that before the beginning of time God predetermined the fate of all mankind, choosing some to be saved and leaving the rest in their depraved state; that God is justified in doing this since all are depraved and it is out of His love and mercy that He saves some from the depraved masses. This choice of who was to be saved or who was not was made before Adam and Eve were created, God forseeing they would sin, and because of that sin all mankind would be totally depraved.

It would benefit the reader to examine how this total depravity would be expressed through the masses of depraved peoples apart from Christianity. The world has certainly experienced the atrocities and heinous acts that have been committed against humanity through the centuries, acts so terrible that they are condemned by societies on a global basis. These acts would bear out the fact of total depravity if they were to be used as the standard. However, the study of history and present day societies will reveal that this type of behavior is minimal in ratio to the masses of peoples. There are many who have lived exemplary moral lives, doing all manner of good for the society in which they live. Disregarding Christians, who are expected to do good, many individuals have sacrificed their lives to serve the needs of others. If all are totally depraved, why are there varying degrees of good and varying degrees of evil? Are there measures of total depravity? Under the concept of total depravity all would be totally lacking of any good and would live an unrestrained life of evil.

If it were true, as Calvinists teach, all born after Adam would be born totally depraved, never having a choice to be otherwise, and yet God would create mankind knowing that great masses would go to Hell where they would live in extreme torment for eternity. The God of Calvinism would have designed a system where He preordained that when, not if, the man He created sinned, He would hold him and all men guilty without offering them a chance for redemption. That god could not be characterized as being loving, merciful, kind or compassionate. Neither could He be thought just, because He willingly created a system that doomed many to Hell without any hope. Just the opposite would be true, such a god would have none of these qualities. The undeniable fact would be that their God willfully created masses of people just to go to Hell. He did this knowing that many He was creating would be eternally tormented and still He created them for such a fate without giving them a choice for redemption. This is certainly not the God described in the scriptures and exemplified by the life of Jesus whose primary mission was to show mankind what God was like. The scriptures actually states that prior to the giving of the law, sin was not imputed to mankind. If it was not imputed by God, why would He condemn them? (Romans 5:13)

Many intelligent men of God embrace this harsh doctrine of predestination. Their conclusions are birthed out of the irrefutable fact that God is sovereign and whatever He chooses to do is appropriate and just. It is also an irrefutable fact that God must first approach man and enlighten him before the man can respond and then, only after God gives him faith. This is indeed a work that can be attributed only to God. Man does not have the power nor wisdom to save himself. Very few theologians would argue this biblical truth. If left only to this knowledge of God, then most would conclude that this doctrine of predestination is indeed valid. The truth is that this picture of a harsh, unloving, unmerciful God does not in any way project the loving image that Jesus portrayed of the Father. This picture does not align with the acts of mercy that Jesus (God) demonstrated to all, not just the elect. This picture fails to accurately present the heart of One who loved the lost of the world so much that He would give His Son so that all could be forgiven of all sin and receive mercy. This picture dismisses the fact that He is not willing that any should perish, that all who will may come. It also dismisses the fact that this loving God is able of predestinating a plan of redemption that includes all the lost. The scriptures are very clear that Jesus died for all sins of all people. The Calvinist position that He only died for those who had been predestined to be saved is not consistent with the New Covenant teachings. Clearly, the scriptures teach differently.

The Bible states that the grace of God that brings salvation has appeared to all men, teaching them to live soberly. Why would a God who had predestined a person for Hell appear to that person at all? If God declares that it is not His will that any should perish and that whosoever will may come, and then does not give those individuals an opportunity to respond to salvation, He would be in violation of His own word. For Him to say that it is not His will for any to perish and then predestine some men to perish without a choice would again be a contradiction both of His character and word.

Those that believe in the total depravity of man and the selective predestination of some to Hell and others to Heaven maintain that the shedding of the blood of Jesus only included those who are chosen. The scriptures declare in several places that Jesus died for all the sins of mankind forever; That our sins are as far as the East is from the West; that through Jesus God has reconciled the world to Himself; that He remembers our sins no longer.

Starting with the premise that God predetermined before time the fate of all mankind, one must conclude that God made this choice apart from any and all other inputs, that nothing following this choice could change the outcome. That being true, there was no valid reason for Jesus to come to earth. His death on the cross could not have an effect upon the predestined choice of God since this was already a settled issue. There could be no redemptive purpose for Jesus' death. To believe otherwise would be to acknowledge that somehow the death of Jesus did have an effect on who was to be saved and, if so, the belief that God had already preordained all who were to be saved would be an untenable position.

Under this type of doctrine it would be foolish to have churches and individuals to demonstrate the Christian life or preach the gospel (good news). What is good about knowing that you are preselected for a destiny for which you have no choice? No amount of teaching or preaching could persuade a non-elect to become an elect. No amount of reasoning could change the outcome of God's choice. Their destiny has already been decided apart from anything they can do, good or evil.

In an effort to explain the scriptures regarding preaching, individual choices, individual responsibility, the atonement of Jesus, and other scriptures relating to salvation as an individual choice, Calvinists say that it was necessary for Jesus to die for the elect. Why if they were already chosen prior to the coming of Christ? It would be foolishness for Jesus to have to die for those that God had already predetermined would be saved. What was the purpose? No, Jesus did not have to come and die if it was predestined who was to be chosen without a choice by man.

Why would Jesus need to die for something that was already decided before hand? Why would an all-knowing God, determine before men were ever created who was to be saved and who was to be left to their depraved state, then design a plan that would include the death of the One He loved so that His choice would be justified?

Since the choice was made prior to man being created, it could have nothing to do with the depraved state of the person, but all to do with the sovereignty of God. The answer cannot be the foreknowledge of God, because God foreknew all men, as none had been born yet. In this scenario, it was not a matter of who God foreknew would respond and who would not since all were depraved and unable to respond. The choice was completely God's, without any man having anything to do with his birth, depravity or choice of destiny. Foreknowledge is man's word that attempts to describe previous knowledge of an event prior to the event happening. Actually, God does not exist on a timeline that includes past, present, and future. He exist always in the present now.

God has given Christians the responsibility to take the gospel to the world. However, if God has already chosen who is to be saved, why would there be a need for churches, missionaries, evangelists or teachers of the gospel? Calvinists teach that since we do not know who the elect are, we must preach the gospel so the ones that are chosen can respond. This view seems to undermine the sovereign choice of God, if a person must respond. Regardless of how many years a person may cultivate another to be saved, if that person is not one of the elect, all his efforts are futile. The other side of the coin would also be true, no amount of denying God, His existence or His love could prevent one of the elect from coming. One must spin an entangled web of misinterpretations of a myriad of scriptures in order to sustain such a doctrine. If a person must respond to an evangelistic message, then he has a choice. The responsibility for them becoming saved then rests with the preachers and teachers of the gospel and not on the preselection of God. If the gospel has to be preached to mankind before they can respond and be saved is necessary, then the outcome depends upon men taking the gospel to every man, woman, and child in order for them to know what they must do to be saved. The individual must also have the ability to respond. This certainly cannot be defined as preselection without choice. Why send missionaries to all corners of the earth if God has already predestined the outcome? Why have evangelists if what they are preaching does not determine who will be saved or not? Why have churches to teach all the wonderful things of the scriptures when it all is a waste of time if God has already predetermined the destiny of all mankind? No amount of preaching can persuade a non-elect to be saved. No amount of witnessing will lead a non-elect to Christ, they are already doomed. The opposite is also true. No amount of warnings about Hell and the judgement of almighty God against their lifestyle of sin will keep them from going to Heaven because it has nothing to do with their sinful lifestyle but the choice of God. Calvinists would say that God's foreknowledge would allow Him to choose properly, but their basic doctrine is that all men are depraved and have no desire for God nor propensity for good. Again, the Calvinist will say that all these scriptural teachings of salvation, evangelizing, teaching the Bible, etc. are true because they must somehow acknowledge that there is a purpose for the recording of these works of God. They say in His sovereignty He has chosen this means to save men. It is inconceivable to believe that an omniscient God would preselect the destiny of all mankind, then design such a meaningless plan for the salvation of those already selected to be saved. The simple truth is that God would need none of these if it were His divine plan to predestine salvation apart from any involvement of mankind. If that were true then all the wonderful truths regarding the love of God and His salvation are just a fairy tale.

- 2 Peter 3:9 - The Lord is not slack concerning His promise, as some count slackness but is long suffering toward us, not willing that <u>any</u> should perish but <u>all</u> should come to repentance. (Emphasis mine)

There would be no need to be long suffering if He has already predestined that a person is forever lost. Why be long suffering if He has already determined who is saved before time began? Long suffering only makes sense if He is granting more time to individuals so that they can respond and be saved.

"<u>Not His will that any should perish but that ALL should come to repentance</u>". The interpretative words for this verse are "any" and "all" If it is not His will that "any" should perish then it must be His will that "all" have opportunity to be saved. It can not be both ways. He can not have a will that chooses some to go to Hell and at the same time have a will that He does not wish any should perish. If He alone has the power to save and if He has already predetermined the fate of all, why would He say that it is not His will that any should perish? If He predetermines some to Hell it would certainly be his will for some to perish. If it is not His will that any should perish and many do perish, there must be a choice the individual can make to circumvent the will of God. The consistent scriptural view of this verse would include John 3:16 and many others that correctly identify God as a loving, long suffering, merciful, kind, and benevolent person who, in His great love and mercy, sent His Son to open the gate of salvation so that whosoever will may come. But He did not just leave mankind on his own to choose, He sent the Holy Spirit to enlighten men and draw them to God. He then furnishes them with the grace and faith to respond. Hallelujah!!!

- Titus 2:11 - For the grace of God that brings salvation has appeared to all men. (Why does a God who has already predetermined who is to be saved and who is to remain lost still present people with the grace that enables them to be saved? Why present grace to those who have no capacity to respond)?

- 1 Timothy 2:3-4 - For this is good and acceptable in the sight of God our Savior, who desires all men to come to the knowledge of the truth. (If God desires ALL men to come to the knowledge of the truth then they must have a choice).

- Ezekiel 18:23 - Do I have any pleasure at all that the wicked should die?

- Ezekiel 18:32 - "For I have no pleasure in the death of one who dies....

- Is it possible that a God who has no pleasure in the death of the wicked would knowingly predestine them to such a place as Hell?

- Matthew 25:41- states that Hell was prepared for the devil and his angels, not as a place to send depraved men.

- Hebrews 10:12 - But this man, after He had offered one sacrifice for <u>sins</u>.

- Hebrews 10: 17 - Then He adds, "their sins and lawless deeds I will remember no more".

- Hebrews 10:18 - Now where there is remission of these, there is no longer an offering for sin.

- John 1:29 - The next day John saw Jesus coming toward him, and said, "Behold! The Lamb of God who <u>takes away the sin of the world.</u> (Emphasis mine)

- 1 John 2:2 - And He Himself is the propitiation for our sins, <u>AND NOT FOR OURS ONLY BUT ALSO FOR THE WHOLE WORLD.</u> (Emphasis mine)

- 2 Corinthians 5:18 - Now all things are of God who has reconciled us to Himself through Jesus Christ, and has given us the ministry of reconciliation.

- The question arises here that if God has already chosen the elect what is the purpose of a ministry of reconciliation? He clearly states what this ministry is in verse 19.

- 2 Corinthians 5:19 - that is, that God was in Christ reconciling the WORLD to Himself, not imputing their trespasses to them, and has committed to us the word of reconciliation.

Two truths emerge here. (1) God's plan through the death of Jesus on the cross was to reconcile the lost world to Himself. We place our salvation on the fact that what Jesus came to do, He completed. If He only died for the elect why would God say that the purpose of His son coming was to make things right between God and the lost world? Jesus did all that was necessary for every person to be able to come to God. God left no walls erected between Himself and lost mankind. This does not mean, as the Universalists teach, that all men are saved. There still remains the response of the individual to the invitation to believe in Jesus. (2) If God is not imputing sin to the lost, then He would be unjust to send individuals to Hell because of their depraved condition without giving them a choice. According to this scripture, all the trespasses of the lost are not imputed or charged to them. If they have been forgiven by God are they still considered depraved by the God who forgave them of the sins?

- John 1:12 – "But as many as received Him, to them He gave the right to become children of God, to those who believe in His name". (He came to His own people and they rejected Him but as many as did believe He made children of God. This does not say as many as were elected).

- John 3:16 – "..that WHOEVER believes in Him should not perish but have everlasting life'. (The truth revealed in this famous scripture has given comfort to men through the years because it states that because God loved the lost world so much He gave His only son as a sacrifice so that whoever from the lost world would believe in Jesus could and would be saved. God preordained and predestined this to be true). (Emphasis mine)

- John 5:24 – "Most assuredly, I say to you, "he who hears My word and believes in Him who sent Me has everlasting life, and shall not come into judgment, but has passed from death into life". (Jesus is emphatic in this statement, the person who believes what He taught about God would receive everlasting life". This verse not only states the person has a choice but adds credence to the mandate to take the gospel into all the world).

- Romans 10:13 – "For whoever calls on the name of The Lord shall be saved". (Again it appears that WHOEVER calls on the name of Jesus will be saved). (Emphasis mine)

- Acts 2:21 – "And it shall come to pass that WHOEVER calls on the name of The Lord shall be saved". (Whoever calls on the name of The Lord, not will be, but shall be saved. It appears that choices are involved.(Emphasis mine)

God's good plan of redemption even makes allowance for little children not yet old enough to choose.

- 2 Samuel 12: 23 - But now he is dead; why should I fast? Can I bring him back again? I shall go to him, but he shall not return to me.

David had fasted in the hope that God would allow his son to live but when his son had died he stated that his dead son could not return from where he had gone after he had died, but that he could go to where his son was. We must conclude that if David went to Paradise and then to Heaven that his son did also.

Jesus declares that little children have angels that behold the face of God. In saying this He included all children not just some who were the elect.

- Matthew 18:10 - Take heed that you do not despise one of these little ones, for I say to you that in Heaven their angels always see the face of My Father who is in heaven.

Jesus is speaking of little children who have no knowledge of sin. In the doctrine of predestination they would be depraved and justly deserving of Hell and yet Jesus declares that they have angels that see the face of God. Scripture does not state nor infer that the depraved have angels that tend to them. It does infer that those who inherit salvation have ministering angels (Hebrews 1:14). It would appear that

God's plan preordained all children for salvation until they come to a place to reject Him. In another place He rebukes some by saying, "Let the little children come to Me, and do not forbid them; for of such is the Kingdom of Heaven"(Matthew 19:14). Other interpretations say that the Kingdom of Heaven belongs to such ones. Jesus seems to be including all little children as having a part in the Kingdom. if so, He has predestined this to be, which contradicts the teaching that He arbitrarily picks some for the kingdom and some for Hell. The love of God would enter all men in His "book of life" until they either rejected Him or died without believing in Him at which time they would be removed from the Book of Life.

- John 3:17 - For God did not send His Son into the world to condemn the world, but that the world through Him might be saved.

What is the conclusion of non-Calvinists-That God created man to love and fellowship with and in His omniscience knew that Adam would fall, affecting all the human race. The Trinity designed a plan for the redemption of all fallen mankind and consummated that plan through the life, death, and resurrection of Jesus, the Son. Through the finished work of Jesus Christ, God extends an invitation to all the lost to become part of His family. Their only requirement is to believe in His Son. God also provides the faith to believe and the grace to respond (Ephesians 2:8-9). It is totally a work of the Spirit of God to bring a person to an understanding of his condition and offer him a chance to be in a relationship with God. The person makes the choice. This is validated through the teachings of Jesus and the epistles. God declares that none will be turned away who come to His Son. God has entrusted this ministry of reconciliation to Christians. They are to proclaim this good news to the lost masses so that they may be saved. God calls His Church to model his Kingdom and teach converts the tenets of the gospel. He has chosen to relate to believers through the New Covenant where He promises to provide, protect, and guide them through life. He has predestined it to be so.

CHAPTER TEN

The Christian's Relationship to the Old Testament Law

During the transition from the law of the Old Covenant, given to Moses on Mt Sinai, to the grace of the New Covenant, provided by Jesus, there was a group of Jews that insisted portions of the law were still required for the new believers. Due to a lack of understanding of the two covenants, this teaching has permeated the doctrines of the Church from its inception to modern times. Most modern churches have adopted some mixture of law into their doctrinal tenets. These written or unwritten requirements have as their basis some form of individual performance and sin management. Granted, many of these requirements originated to assist the individual in maintaining a righteous lifestyle and project an acceptable Christian image. However, as well meaning as the motives may be, the end result is the same, bondage to a set of performance laws. Where these requirements exist, the simplicity and purity of grace is compromised. To enjoy the freedoms provided under the New Covenant of grace, the Church must adopt the same radical safeguards taught by the Apostle Paul in his epistles. Paul is emphatic that the requirements of the Law were fulfilled in Christ Jesus and have no control over the Christian.

The Law had both a purpose and perimeters. From the time of Adam until the giving of the law to Moses, acts of sin existed in the world, but they were not imputed as sin because they had not been identified by God as sin. God rectified this with the giving of the Law on Mt. Sinai. With the Law, God established perimeters as to who was required to keep the Law and what they were required to keep. The Law was God's covenant with the nation of Israel and did not apply to any of the gentile nations. The mainstay of the Law was the Ten Commandments, but it also included which foods were acceptable to eat, civil laws that governed their relationships to each other, moral laws that established perimeters of righteous living and sacrificial laws that governed how their sins were to be atoned.

Although the Law was given specifically for Israel, it is highly beneficial to the Christian, because it identifies areas of sin. Although all sin has been forgiven, there remains the harmful result of sin. The Law acts as a standard of righteousness for lost gentiles and Jews alike. It is the standard for all who believe that they are able by their own acts of righteousness or beliefs in a religious system to attain eternal life and a place in Heaven. It is impossible for any person to keep the 613 tenets of the law. Animal sacrifices would have ceased if Israel had been able to keep the Law. By the standard of the Law none will be justified before God. Therefore the Law becomes a tutor to lead one to Christ. The Law identifies the ungodly and unholy. Christ has redeemed us from the Law and made us to be the righteousness of God.

Animal sacrifice was the means which allowed violators of the Law to escape punishment for their sins. Because it was inevitable that the people would continue to sin, it was necessary for the sacrifice of animals to continue from year to year. When an animal was to be sacrificed, it was the animal, not the person bringing the animal, that was examined to determine if it was an accepted sacrifice. If the animal was accepted, the person bringing the animal was accepted.

These animal sacrifices were a type pointing to the reality of the coming of the unblemished Lamb of God, who takes away all the sins of the world, once for all time, so that a sinful world could be forgiven and fellowship be restored with a Holy God. We have been made acceptable because Jesus was the accepted sacrifice for our sins.

Although Jesus has fulfilled the law and frees the Christian from its dictates, the Law still speaks to those that willingly or ignorantly place themselves under any portion of the Law.

- Romans 3:19 – Now we know that whatever the law says, it says to those who are under the law.

The term "under the law" means that if a person places himself under the Law, then the Law is speaking to him. If he is listening to what the Law says and is obeying it, then it is speaking to him. If a person is listening to the Law, then it governs his life. What is the Law saying to those under the law? It is defining good and evil, what is acceptable and what is not acceptable. The Law then judges a person's actions and thoughts to see if he has perfectly obeyed its demands. If he has failed, then the Law passes judgment upon him and condemns him.

The Law is a ministry of death and condemnation because it was specifically designed to reveal the heart of man and his inability to attain the righteousness required by a holy God (2 Corinthians 3:6-8).

Paul warns the Galatians that if they desire to keep one aspect of the Law then they must keep all the Law. To violate one is to violate all. To keep one, all must be kept. If one desired to be circumcised then he must also keep the entire Law (Galatians 5:1-4) (James 2:10).

Paul also warns that to try to justify ourselves by following the Law causes us to be estranged from Christ and causes us to fall from grace. It is obvious that he is not talking about losing our salvation but falling back under the law. When a person willingly places himself back under the law that Christ died to free him from, he denies and rejects the benefits of grace.

There are many entanglements with the Law that are subtle and appeal to the Christian because they provide a perceived form of righteousness and because they were valid under the old covenant. Some include the observance of Jewish rituals and dress as a means of better identifying with Christ. These rituals were valid in their time because they were a picture of Christ. However, we have the reality, which is Christ. Why continue to embrace a type or shadow when we can embrace the substance, Christ? Paul sternly rebukes the Galatians for reverting back to the Law after receiving the Spirit by faith (Galatians 3:1-3).

Although the Old Covenant has been made obsolete and terminated by God Himself, the Law continues to serve a valid purpose. We, as Christians, are freed from the Law, and it no longer applies to us. However, the Law is holy and will remain in effect as long as individuals believe they can attain righteousness through their works or status, as long as individuals or groups believe they can reach heaven by their good works, as long as religions believe they can circumvent a belief in the Son of God for their salvation, and as long as men establish their own standard for righteousness. Jesus said that not one jot or tittle of the Law would pass away.

It is both refreshing and liberating knowing that, as Christians, we are not bound to the Law. The righteousness required by the Law has been given to us as a gift under grace. Now we live from the basis of being righteous not following a list of rules to attain righteousness.

-   "For the law was given through Moses, but grace and truth came through Jesus Christ" (John 1:17). (God wrote the Law on a stone with His finger and gave it to Moses for the people of Israel. The Law became the parameters of the Old Covenant. But God expressed His grace and truth through His Son (just the selection of the messengers should show us which was the more important).

-   Romans 8:1-4 ....for what the law could not do in that it was weak through the flesh, God did by sending His own Son in the likeness of sinful flesh, on account of sin: He condemned sin in the flesh.

-   Romans 8:4 – That the righteous requirements of the law might be fulfilled in *us* who do not walk according to the flesh but according to the Spirit.

- Colossians 2:8 - Beware lest anyone cheat you through philosophy and empty deceit, according to the traditions of men, according to the basic principles of the world, and not according to Christ.

- Colossians 2:13 – And you, being dead in your trespasses and the uncircumcision of your flesh. He has made alive together with Him, having forgiven you all trespasses.

- Colossians 2:14 – having wiped out the handwriting of requirements that was against us, which was contrary to us. And He has taken it out of the way, having nailed it to the cross.

- 2 Corinthians 3:6 –Who also made us sufficient as minister of the new covenant; not of the letter but of the Spirit; for the letter kills but the Spirit gives life.

God has written His laws in our mind and on our heart. These laws are not the Ten Commandments because they were made obsolete as recorded in Hebrews 8:13. God would not write something on our heart that was no longer valid, that was a ministry of death and condemnation, Therefore, these have to be the laws of grace.

"Many people see the cross only as an act of divine justice. To satisfy his need for justice, God imposed the ultimate punishment on his Son, thus satisfying his wrath and allowing us to go unpunished. That may be good news for us, but what does it say about God? His wrath wasn't an expression of the punishment sin deserves; it was the antidote for sin and shame. His plan was not just to provide a way to forgive sin, but to destroy it so that we might live free. Don't think God was only a distant spectator that day. He was in Christ reconciling the world to Himself. This is something they did together. This was not some sacrifice God required in order to be able to love us, but a sacrifice God himself provided for what we needed. He leaped in front of a stampeding horse and pushed us to safety. He was crushed by the weight of our sin so that we could be rescued from it. It's an incredible story."
— Wayne & Dave Jacobsen

Conclusion: Jesus paid it all, all to Him I owe. Sin had left a crimson stain; He washed it white as snow. Jesus fulfilled the Law in our place; therefore we are not under the dictates of the Law. Christ has paid the penalty for all our sins, and God does not impute acts of sin against us. If God does not ascribe our acts of wrong doings as sins, He declares us to be righteous and not sinful. If God does not hold us accountable for sin it is as if we do not sin. Does that mean that we can indulge in the works of the flesh without consequence, of course not! Although God does not condemn us, there are always adverse effects that accompany acts of wrong doing. God clearly defines the works of the flesh as well as the fruit of the Spirit. He warns against the works of the flesh and elevates the fruit of the Spirit. Works of the flesh are clearly those thoughts, attitudes and actions that are performed outside the parameters of grace, while the fruit of the spirit man is obviously performed through enabling grace (Galatians 5:19-23 describe the works of the flesh versus the fruit of the Spirit).

My prayer is that this book has caused you to have "aha" experiences that have enriched your understanding of the marvelous gift of God's grace. I pray that it has further encouraged you to mine the scriptures for the many treasures of His grace; treasures that He has predestined for us to receive and enjoy.